MY FATHER'S
DAUGHTER

LORETTA ODUWARE OGBORO-OKOR

i

Published & Printed In Nigeria

BookSale:
3A, Ajoke Okusanya, Off Abel Oreniyi,
Off Salvation Rd, Opebi, Ikeja. Lagos, Nigeria.

www.booksale.com.ng

Cover Design:
Peters Owolabi

FOREWORD

I first encountered the force of nature otherwise known as Loretta Ogboro-Okor, just under 18 months ago at an event in Manchester, United Kingdom. The event was convened to discuss ideas of tackling the difficult subject of 'Edo Women' trafficking to Italy. I am truly delighted I attended the event, even though I initially turned down the invitation, as I am an extremely busy. However after a strong and emotive persuasion from the influential and charismatic organizer I accepted the invitation, and agreed to host the day. Now, in hindsight, I know it was no random coincidence I agreed.

My first recollection of Loretta was of a beautiful, demure and graceful looking woman in that combination, as she spoke with several guests. However when I handed her the microphone to deliver her short 20 minutes speech, I was in for a shock. As a matter of fact the entire room full of people was held spell bound! The room literally erupted as Loretta commanded the room mainly with her unencumbered, passionate and spirited delivery. She challenged everyone to do something about the evils of this particular trade, and the effects on the women and girls involved. She used emotive language and tugged at the heartstrings of everyone, leaving so many in awe, with their hearts ablaze, as she commanded the room.

Loretta spoke with so much authority as one who understands intrinsically what can happen to a person without the right substratum of identity, support, courage, self-esteem, self-belief and strong convictions instilled in them.

Loretta and I instantly connected and we have been friends ever since. That trip to Manchester for me I suspect was mainly to meet Loretta and get another glimpse at life through her own life experiences. Since I ply my trade as an inspirational leadership speaker, providing training to corporations internationally, teaching 'best practice' and success strategies for lasting success, I value the meeting of minds.

So when I was approached by Loretta to write the forward for her book aptly titled - 'MY FATHER'S DAUGHTER', I was deeply honoured.

Now to this beautifully written, short and easy to read book, replete with anecdotes from a truly challenging life of this inimitable author in her usual unapologetic style, we find a treasure throve of commanding counsel and sage advice for anyone raising children, especially female children. More poignantly the heart of this book is concentrated on 'Pa. Richard' the man who did an unsurpassed job of raising this beautiful lady. He loaded her with social and life transforming codes of etiquette, which have sustained her and continues to see her through turbulent phases of her life!

Without giving away too much, as you the reader delve into the pages of this short book, you will find yourself making mental adjustments, and challenging yourself to rise to a higher standard of parenthood or guardian. You will find yourself gleaning wisdom of what to incorporate and praying it is not too late for you to do so. Even if you should find it too late for your own biological children, you will also see the wisdom as a collective of how to contribute to the wider society.

I cannot underestimate the importance of fathers especially, to infuse life into their daughters. The active presence and love of a father can powerfully influence a child's cognitive, social, and emotional development.

A father's influence and direct involvement with encouragement will help to diminish a girl child's insecurity and raise her self-esteem.

As a dad of a 12 year old girl myself, I know the importance and power of a father's affirmation. Having read this book, I have discovered from the example of late Pa Richard that I have not done well enough.

This book is for everyone, boys to learn importance lessons of how to be a man, Men to understand their responsibilities as the foundational strength of society, and how to use their power more responsibly. Girls will learn how to grow into self-respecting women with grace and women will learn vital lessons in raising their children with strength.

I whole-heartedly recommend this powerful book, and my eternal thanks and appreciations go to this uncommon author Dr. Loretta Ogboro-Okor.

Charles Ajayi-Khiran,
Inspirational Leadership Speaker,
Trainer & Coach,
Author 'The Entrepreneur's Code'
26th June, 2018.

DEDICATION

To my father who taught me to "dine with Kings and eat with Paupers" his words to me verbatim.

To my mum, who nurtured me with love and grace un-paralleled.

To my husband, in whom I am well pleased.

To my children, who continue to help me connect life's dots.

To all my siblings who I have the privilege of sharing my father with - I love you all.

To all my friends, too numerous to mention especially Chikodi Ezewungo, Ayo Itoya, Aize Okojie-Iyamu, Micheal Achile Umameh, Belo Utoblo, Winifred Osakwe- Kokroko, Omoyemwen Agbonwanegbe-Okogwu, Erhio Obodo, Ava Brown, Ufuoma nee Okparanyote, Ufuoma Okotete-Awomosu, Iguehi Obokhare, Deborah Laogun and Jojo Ighodaro; you all are the wind beneath my wings.

To my haters, I salute you all. I am indebted to you, for it is because of the likes of you and the challenges you brought along my path, that I rise.

PROLOGUE

I am my father's daughter. I am unapologetic about it.

The rain poured down from the heavens like a hole had suddenly come unplugged by the creator, from where huge unending drums of water poured onto the red earth associated with Benin City.

Benin, the ancient city of the Ogisos, the land of the Obas, home to a people of heritage so rich in culture that their tales of splendour abound on the internet and in history books. The relics of their civilization grace our galleries as well as the museums of other countries across the world - treasures taken without the consent of the original Benin owners. Suffice it to say we shall come back to the matter of heritage. Let us focus on the father and his daughter who are at the centre of this narrative for now.

Through that rain and the red muddy flood it created, waded a man with grey hair determined to get to the school. The taxi he came in was unable to navigate the flooded road, a few meters before the school gate. Nothing was going to stop him!

When he set out on this journey, his car had broken down, but he was not deterred as he was on a mission to pick his children from school. They would be waiting and he was not one to let his children down. So he got his long time taxi driver friend at an added cost to ferry him to the school. He had picked the two younger children and was yet to pick the oldest of the three. The flood could not deter him as he jumped out of the taxi and made his way through the muddy road to the school gate. That was my father: Richard Harold Osaroguiwa Ogboro. In empathy with the readers of this book, who will consider his name a tongue twister of which we his children are proud, I will stick to Pa. Richard when not calling him daddy or father henceforth.

I was sitting in my classroom with my classmates who had the look of uncertainty plastered on their faces. Due to the adverse weather condition, they wondered when they would eventually get to their individual homes, considering that the rain was not abating. I remained unflustered and calm; an onlooker might even have mistaken my look to be a happy one!

The forlorn look on the face of our class teacher who had given up the task of trying to predict when she would get to the comfort of her home was now obvious for all of us to see. She was bothered because she was only going to be able to leave after every single child had been picked up by their parents or guardians. Her sober look did not bother me either. I remained happy and expectant to the amazement of others around me. The reason for my annoying joy was the simple fact I knew my father would come. Even if the world was coming to an end, daddy was going to come. He never failed me, not once and what is more? Daddy kept his words; his word was his bond. He had told me earlier that morning he would pick me up. Even the heaviest tears of nature would not deter my father from keeping his promise. Of that I was certain, for he taught me how to keep my word against all odds. At every slight opportunity he had, he found a way to show me how important it is to maintain one's integrity even when that was the road least travelled. He also taught me how not to seek external validation and pander to the influences of others at the expense of my own beliefs.

I knew my daddy would come. My daddy came. In the rain! He defied the flood. He was allowed into the classroom since we were not able to go outside. Ever the gentleman, Pa. Richard greeted the entire class and the teacher, remarking that the weather would get better and more parents would soon turn up. His words of encouragement cheered them up while I picked my school bag and hurried out with my daddy with a smug smile of satisfaction plastered on my face - I knew Pa. Richard would come, and he came!

I find it remarkable that I have a recollection of my Nursery and Primary school events until date. The first challenge I encountered when I decided it was time to put down the chronicles of my life in print was the sheer volume of information that rushed at me from my years of sojourn on earth. The ultimate question was, how do write it all down? For many years I struggled with this inertia while carrying about volumes in my mind until the day I decided to do it. It is only fair that in today's world where many find it hard to get a role model and positive influence, those of us who had one should be kind enough to share our experiences.

There is no such thing as a perfect life or a perfect upbringing. However, in hind sight, I have come to realise that the appreciation of what one has, is the measure of perfection and not the other way round. I appreciate the parents who raised me and looking back, I have not turned out badly. It is my prayer that everyone who interacts with this piece of work finds something within it that ministers to their needs, answers their questions or inadequacies and that they become better after reading it.

I am my father's daughter. I am unapologetic about it.

MEET THE MAN

It will be good for me to let you in on my father's heritage at this point. This is to enable a connection with his background and see the world from his side of the pond. I often say we are a sum total of our life experiences and exposures, therefore a glimpse into the roots of Pa. Richard will enhance a visualisation of the man and why he developed the lifestyle he did. It will give the reader a better template on which to access and assess the man, the father and the mentor.

He was born a Prince, yet he lived for the people, dined with the people and wined with kings. A man who caught on a bit late in life but eventually came to self-actualisation at a very rapid pace far beyond his peers.

He was born in 1920 to a father who understood the meaning of pampering his children and living life to the full. Prince Richard Harold Osaroguiwa Ogboro, my father, was the son of Erhabor Osagiede Ogboro who hailed from the famous Ogboro family in Ogbe Quarters, Benin City. Erhabor Osagiede Ogboro was one of the early Benin men to interact with the colonials and other tribes across Nigeria. He was a man of great affluence and influence because he worked with the then colonial administrator of the old Oyo province and the Public Works Department in Calabar as a contractor for many years.

These interactions during his life sojourn outside his native land of Benin City were to have strong influence on how he lived his life without stereotypes and most importantly how he raised his children- my father and his siblings. This by extension gave rise to the many positive legacies he bequeathed to his future generations. Erhabor educated and pampered all his children of which Richard Osaroguiwa Ogboro was the first son.

Sometimes after my father told me stories of how my grandfather used to dispose of all his clothes annually and get new ones. I marvelled at what would have been a unique style and great taste in fashion displayed by my ancestor, even at the time.

Richard was the product of his marriage to Princess Ohonbie Josephine Usunalele Ovonranmwen, who was the first grandchild of Omo n'Oba n'Edo, Uku Akpolokpolo, Oba Ovonranmwen ne Ogbaisi, the 36th Oba of Benin; who was deported to Calabar by the British following their infamous invasion of his Kingdom in 1897. Princess Ohonbie was the first child of Prince Usunalele Ovonranmwen of Ibiwe Quarters.

It may interest you to know that this woman who eventually became the mother of Prince Richard H. Osaroguiwa Ogboro (who would in turn become my father) was with her grandfather Oba Ovoranmwen in Calabar, when the British exiled him. She lived in Calabar, with her grandfather, where he spent his last days and eventually passed on to the land of his ancestors.

Uvbie Primary School, which was near her old abode on First East Circular Road in Benin, was named after her. A devout Catholic and a frequent face at the St. Joseph's Catholic Church in her time, it was said that there were times she entered the Oba's Palace and her first cousin, Oba Akenzua II would ensure all traditional proceeding and drumming's were put to a halt while she was around so as not to offend the deep sense of Catholicism she had come to adopt.

So it was, that Richard Harold Osaroguiwa Ogboro was birthed by two persons of unique pedigree. Something he never lost sight of in his entire lifetime judging by the way he conducted his affairs with strict decorum and a confidence that comes from knowing who he was.

In spite of this, those who knew him have always reiterated his humility – some described him as a paradox: a man full of self-confidence that bordered on self- pride who simultaneously displayed unparalled humility all his life.

Okoro (Prince) Richard Ogboro attended Government School in Benin City. He went on to Methodist Boys High School Oron in present day Akwa Ibom State. Going to high school did not come naturally to Richard. He recounted to me in his lifetime, how he was initially content to enjoy the attention of his community who made him feel like a hero, eulogising him as to his pedigree. He described how he used to watch his mother cry and pray daily that her son should come to see the light and go to high school.

He told me how his light bulb moment came when his peers who had gone to boarding houses came back home during the holidays and looked down on him with superior aloofness. That was all he needed to galvanize him into action. He was not going to sit down and allow any one talk down on him. He knew he had to do something and quick too. He had been too nonchalant about the direction his life was taking for too long. Now he was going to take the reins. Indeed, his mother's prayers must have become sweet smelling to the heavens!

He went to his mother and told her he was ready to go to school. There was no turning back... he became a man determined to make up for the earlier time lost and completely overhauled his approach to life. He worked hard to become one of the first crop of Nigerians to obtain a fellowship with the Royal Society of Health Inspectors Education.

He was eventually sponsored by the World Health Organisation to attend Durham University in Newcastle and Oklahoma State University in the United States of America where he obtained his training as a Sanitary Health Engineer and Public Health Consultant.

He rose to become the Head of the Epidemiology Unit of the Ministry of Health Benin City, in the then Bendel State of Nigeria. Pa. Richard became dedicated to the service of humanity with a determination to maintain value for human life for his people at all levels. He was constantly on the move working in regions across the old Midwestern region: Burutu, Bomadi, Forcados, Auchi, spreading the good news of Public Health and Preventive Medicine at the grass root.

He founded and became the first foundation acting Principal and Instructor of the School of Health Technology at Dumez Road in Benin City, Edo State. He founded and was Head of the Malaria Eradication/Control Unit of the Ministry of Health in Bendel State. He did his job with the singular dedication of one who attached value to human life. He was reputed as the man who would neither 'accept a bribe' nor 'compromise his dignity'. A man who stood for the truth at all times. He retired as Chief Health Officer of the old Bendel State in Nigeria.

Pa. Richard's life summary shows a man with pedigree, who had self-developed and 'conquered himself' over time. There is none without their flaws. My father had his flaws. I know them and I will explore them in the course of this book. We even discussed them and I often told him that I learnt as much from his flaws as I learnt from his strengths. His upbringing; having an affluent father who showered his children with love, set the stage for the way Pa. Richard in-turn treated his own children.

This is based on the simple phenomenon I have come to discover in life, which is, "we cannot give what we do not have. What we have not acquired in the journey of our lives, we do not have a reservoir of and we cannot give out what is not stored in our tanks".

ERHABOR OSAGIEDE OGBORO
My paternal grandfather.

PRINCESS OHONBIE JOSEPHINE USUNALELE

*The first grandchild of Omo n'Oba n'Edo,
Uku Apolokpolo, Oba Ovonranmwen ne Ogbaisi,
the 36th Oba of Benin Kingdom.
My paternal grandmother*

PRINCE (OKORO) RICHARD HAROLD
OSAROGUIWA OGBORO.
My Father

PRINCE USUNALELE OVONRANMWEN
*The son of Oba Ovonranmwen
and father of my grandmother*

ERHABOR OSAGIEDE OGBORO
*This is another picture of my
paternal grandfather*

OMO N'OBA N'EDO, UKU APOLOKPOLO,
OBA OVONRANMWEN NE OGBAISI,
THE 36TH OBA OF BENIN KINGDOM
*The last Soverign monarch of Benin Kingdom
who was deported to Calabar after the
British invasion of Benin in 1897.*

*Father of Prince Usunalele and
my great great grandfather*

8

My Family Line Down The Ages In Collage

Pa. Richard was raised with love. He was exposed to empowerment and understood that the true value of an individual was the net worth of how well the person affected those around him or her positively. At the exact point in his life when he came to all of this realisation, I cannot say. However, I can speak for the time he raised my mother's children and myself. He raised us with love unlimited and invested his time and energy building our self-worth, self-esteem and confidence to the extent that sometimes, even our mother complained that he was not raising us to be compliant with the roles of women in the society. To which my father would always respond that all his children are first human beings and that they could not and will not be limited by gender connotations – no society anywhere in the world was going to rein his daughters in, with tradition or concepts that does not dignify or empower them.

I am my father's daughter. I am unapologetic about it.

THE DAUGHTER

For the purpose of this write up, I will keep as much away from the involvement of all my siblings as I can. I will only narrate events that concern them when it may alter the meaning of those events were they not to be mentioned. The reason for this is because this is my own vision and perception of my experiences through my own eyes and a recollection of all that happened to me. I prefer to maintain their privacy as much as I can and not taint my work with perceptions from them or other relatives who may have lived with us at the time.

I was born on a Saturday evening in the late seventies my father told me. He remembered because it was on his return from the Benin City Rosicrucian Lodge where they had their evening weekly activities that he got the news my mother had delivered a bouncing baby girl. Those were the days before mobile phone technology so he only got to know of events after I was born. He rushed to the hospital, a very happy man.

My mother was not his first wife. I have older half-siblings. He was a Prince of the land and a lot of years older than her. He was better educated in terms of paper certificates and more travelled in terms of exposure. Yet he adored her. My first Ladybird books I read were the ones handed down to me by my mummy. My daddy bought her Ladybird books and started from scratch to teach her to read when they met. She caught up to the point that she was eventually able to secure an appointment in one of the ministries in the state.

However, how they both negotiated the gap in age, education and pedigree was something that fascinated my young mind since then and up till now. When I grew older, I used to jokingly ask my daddy why he married more than one wife. "Why were you a serial monogamist who decided his last bus stop would be my mummy?" I asked him.

His reply was a sad one. He told me how he missed his very first love and how somehow, he was never quite able to replace her. She was a Yoruba lady, this first love of his. His mother, who was a revered Benin Princess in her day, disapproved of her because the lady was from a different tribe. To please his mother, he sought and married a wife from his own tribe. He told me he never quite got it right after that. I told him I have the feeling that if he had married his very first love as he wanted to, I would never have been born. He would smile at me and not respond. I guess he never wanted to hurt anything or anyone, least of all me – hence the reason he chose not to respond to my teasing comments.

One of the first things I remember growing up was my daddy reading us bed time stories. Pa. Richard was dedicated to reading to us. I still think every Ladybird book ever published in his time must have found their way into our home. Remember my mother benefited from them too as I earlier mentioned. The reading sessions were not restricted to bedtime only. They happened anytime my father was not busy reading his own books or doing his own thing. Left to him, he would happily have spent every minute reading to us but he knew better than to make us into 'Jack the dull boy' types. I still recollect how he "opened the door to the world" for me through all kinds of literature. Books, books and more books!

Subjects ranged from religion, history, politics and science to any concept that caught our attention. Pa. Richard started each day listening to British Broadcasting Corporation (BBC) news followed by the Voice of America (VOA) news and next the Nigerian news, all on his radio.

The television news times were also never missed. Therefore, growing up, news was a very potent portion of my life. My siblings and I got used to listening to the news. Initially, we reluctantly listened in but eventually; it became a part of us. On my part, I have never managed to shed my love for news and the desire to be up to date with current world events. I need to know – my father brought me up to be inquisitive. He encouraged us to interrogate our environment and the people around us without fear. He buttressed this by example. I cannot remember any question I asked my father that he did not answer. It did not matter how trivial or how difficult the question appeared to be; he always found the time and patience to answer me.

An example is when we got talking about Malaria once. Yes, you read right. Malaria! You see, he was a Public Health Consultant who rose to become the Head of the Epidemiology Unit of the Ministry of Health Benin City, in the then Bendel State in Nigeria. Malaria still remains a public health problem of great magnitude in world endemic regions like Nigeria.

So it was only natural for us to get into a Malaria discourse. Pa. Richard took time to patiently explain to me, the life cycle of the female Anopheles mosquitoes and the role they play in transmitting Plasmodium falciparum, the unicellular protozoan and parasite that causes Malaria. He explained that the mosquito, in a bid to get a blood meal transmits the parasite from one person to the other.

That was enough to start my barrage of questions. "Why do the mosquitoes require the blood in the first place? Can they not just feed on plant juices?" I asked.

"True there are those that feed on the juices of plants," he explained. "There are different species of mosquitoes. The female Anopheles mosquitoes need the blood meals to develop their eggs. So by proxy, they pick up the parasite, which requires them to complete a part of its life cycle."

"If all you have said is true daddy, then where did the very first mosquito, with the very first Plasmodium parasite come from?" I probed further.

He laughed long and hard then said to me, "You know what Taa, (by the way, that was the version of my name he would often use) this question is one very difficult puzzle. For many years, scientists have struggled to answer this question you are asking, my dear seven-year-old Princess. If I had the answer, I would be able to change the world. I would be able to cure Malaria." The look on his face was one of a man deep in thought. A man, who was truly pondering over the questions of this seven year old and was humble enough to tell her he did not have the answers.

That was my father!

I had the rare privilege from an early age to have conversations with my father like we were equals. He often sought my opinion on different things and once I gave my answer, he would also give his. We would deliberate on both points of views and engage in an in-depth analysis of the pros and cons of both opinions. Most times, I would bow to my father's superior reasoning on many subjects. However, there were times he told me that he believed I had a lot more reasoning packed in my answers than was expected for a child of my age. On such
occasions, he did not hesitate to agree with my point of view. Those were moments that built my confidence beyond what words could describe.

There were times we had to seek answers from the reservoir of knowledge, which was my mummy. She would happily fill the gaps my daddy could not complete. If I wanted to know the names of all the classical musicians, I knew I had to go to my father. On the flip side, for the names of the musicians of the people and clime of the Benins at the time, I would go to my mummy.

The dichotomy between these two became a compensatory

stabilising mechanism for my development. What more could a curious growing child have asked for?

I am my father's daughter. I am unapologetic about it.

WHEN THE FOUNDATION IS ROCK SOLID

I remember it like it was yesterday, the way I was bullied as a child in Primary school. I am lighter skinned than the average black African, a skin complexion I owe to my heritage. I also had large hazel coloured eyes while growing up, protruding upper jaw and teeth from a habit of thumb sucking. Thumb sucking was a habit I developed from infancy and continued up until my late teens. These features became the recipe for other children to bully me in Primary school.

Every day, some 30 children would clap and call me 'yellow pawpaw', 'pussy cat eyes' and 'rabbit teeth'! I started dreading going to school. On one fateful day, when my father came to pick me up and found me in tears, I had to tell him about my predicament. The after-school periods while we waited for our parents or guardians to pick us up were the worst times. In all their idle glory at that time of the day and with very little teacher supervision, the bullies would gang together as if on some uniting psychic cue and begin to taunt me. I would run to a corner and cry, wishing they would stop clapping and singing about my physical features and just go away. For a young child, I began to think I was the problem.

That crucial day, when Pa. Richard came around to pick me from school, my eyes were red. I had been crying. He asked me what the problem was. I told him. I thought he was going to the teachers straight away and get them to caution the students. That was not an option I fancied because that would just draw more attention to me, make the bullies recoup and even enable them recruit more numbers for a perceived weakling and a common enemy. So you can imagine my joy when my daddy smiled and said "Taa, let us go home. We will talk more about this later. However, why did you not let me in on this little issue since?" He asked as we walked towards the car.

One would have thought these are children from respectable homes considering the purported status of this school." He sighed.

When we got home, Pa. Richard called me after my meal, asked me to sit down next to him and recount all that had been happening in school. I told him it began when I started primary school but that it had got worse in the last two years after I got a double promotion to a class above my peers.

He asked me if I had done anything to them to warrant such treatment. "I cannot remember hurting anyone or being mean to any of them daddy," I replied.

My mother who had come into the living room was furious. She wanted to go to the school the next day to confront all the teachers, the children and their parents. How dare they bully her daughter?

"I will slap each and every one of those wicked children tomorrow!" She screamed at the top of her lungs.

My daddy took one look at my mummy and advised her to calm down. "You will do no such thing" he calmly responded.

I thanked my stars that Pa. Richard dissuaded my mother from that line of action. "Now, to you my dear daughter, why do you cry when people call you 'yellow pawpaw', 'pussy cat eyes' and 'rabbit teeth'?"

I stared at my father aghast! I could not understand the man at all.

What sort of question was he asking me? Why shouldn't I cry when I was being called names? What else was I supposed to do? This man was strange, if one is hurt, surely, one was entitled to cry and garner some sympathy?

My hazel eyes got bigger as these thoughts rushed through my mind. Pa. Richard must have read my thoughts. He carried on like I had given voice to them. "Are you not fair skinned? Does that not make you a yellow pawpaw? Are you, my fair angel, not hazel eyed? Does that not make you pussycat eyed? As for your teeth, yes they are protruding and we know why. Just stop sucking your thumb. However, the gap at the diastema makes your smile the prettiest ever. A very pretty rabbit indeed."

I looked at my Dad in amazement!

He looked at me smiling, 'Answer the questions my dear daughter,' he said.

My mother who by now, could neither put up with the slow pace of this discussion nor understand how this was going to bring those tormenting her daughter to justice of any form got impatient.

"How will all these questions help or get them to stop tormenting our child?" she asked.

"I will never understand your methods. I need to attend to the food I am cooking. If anything should happen to my daughter, I will make sure I beat up those children" she screeched and stormed off to the kitchen.

My father remained his calm self. He turned to me and requested me to answer the questions he had asked me earlier. I contemplated his questions for a few minutes as he waited patiently for my response. Then very slowly, I looked him in the eyes and responded, "Daddy, I am fair skinned. Yes. That makes me a yellow –pawpaw. I also have these strange coloured eyes and my teeth and jaw are protruding. Yes!!"

"So, is there anything those children have said that is not true?" Father asked

"No daddy. There is nothing they said that is not true."

"Then why do you cry then, when they say it?" He asked. "Well, I suppose they all say it at once, daddy. All of them, about 30 of them and they shout and clap – taunting me."

"Does your crying stop them?"

"No daddy. In fact, the more I cry, the more they clap and sing."

"So, why cry about what is true anyway? Why cry about your complexion that God has given to you? Or the loveliest pair of large strange coloured eyes on this planet? Or the finest smile I have ever seen?"
I looked at my father, very confused. He stared back at me with eyes of steel, reflecting a determination I had not seen before. Then it dawned on me. I had a light bulb moment. "Daddy, why do I even cry at all if all they say is true?" I asked my father.

"You tell me." He said.
"Daddy, do you really think my skin is pretty? Are my eyes lovely like you said? What about my teeth? Should I wear braces?"

All the questions came rushing out at once. My father smiled. He looked at me, then got up and left the living room. He came back with a mirror. Yes – you read right, a hand held mirror. He pushed it into my hands and told me to take a look at myself. As I looked in the mirror, Pa. Richard began to speak in his calm clear tone.

"You see my daughter, that person you are looking at in the mirror is very special. She is a very unique young girl who will grow into a smart and beautiful lady someday. There is only one of you ever made. There is no other person like you the world over my dear daughter. You are so pretty and important Loretta, (whenever my father used my full name, then he meant business) that some 30 or so children, have to take time out of their learning activities to clap and sing for you and what is more, the song is about you!"

"So what do I do tomorrow when they come at me again?" I asked. "What do you think you should do?" Pa. Richard asked me.

I paused for a while and then smiled. I could see clearly then what I had not seen all this while. I looked at my daddy with a determination that matched his own and replied. "I will never cry again. I am a pretty yellow pawpaw with a lovely smile and eyes. My daddy has told me so and my daddy does not lie."

"Wonderful!" My father remarked.

"Now, that is my girl. You will hold your head high and tell them how happy you are with your skin, eyes and teeth. Tell them how no one else in the world has your kind of eyes, skin or teeth because there is only one of you ever created."

The more my father spoke, the more his words became like opium to me. I suddenly became elated and could not wait for school the next day. I was spared any reading for the day. I was allowed to play to my heart's content before I retired to bed early. Just before I went to bed, daddy came to me to and said: "Remind me to buy you a fountain pen with an inkwell my dear Princess, you deserve it. That is the prize you get for figuring out what to do to your bullies."
"What is a fountain pen?" I asked Pa. Richard.

"You will know what it is when I get you one," my father replied, beaming with an infectious smile.

The next day at school was one I will never forget in my lifetime. I rushed into the class with the eagerness of a scientist who had found the answer to a lifelong experiment. I waited for the bullies. At break time, they came! If you know how bullies work, you will understand, there is always a herald, then the others follow like a pack of wolves. The first one started, "Yellow paw-paw it is break time. What are you reading? I guess you have no one to play with, that's why you are stuck here?" I smiled and stood up majestically, drawing myself to my full height which was quite impressive for my age at the time and when compared to my peers. "You see, I am so happy with myself, my skin, eyes and teeth that I do not need a crowd to make me happy. Where are the rest of your crew? Surely, you need them to help you feel complete, to help you sing and dance for me."

The consternation on his face was marvellous to behold. He could not understand why I was not crying. Why was I standing up? I usually was supposed to start crying and then crouch in a corner like a tiny helpless creature. Then his cohorts would come in and the clapping and singing would begin. The script was not going according to plan that day, which made his confusion palpable.

"Did you say you are happy being a yellow pawpaw?" He asked.

"I am happy being me. I love me. My daddy says I am pretty and since my daddy does not lie, it means you are the one not telling me the truth. Why should I cry anyway? My eyes are strange, which is true. My teeth are protruding yes and my skin is fairer than yours. I know all of these things already and I do not need any of you to tell me what I know. Why should I cry because of these things anyway? Answer me!"

The others had started coming back by this time. They were not sure why their leader was chatting with me. Why is she not crying? They must have wondered. They all looked unsure of what to do. In no time, break was over, my newly found strategy worked and I had escaped! Soon it would be another critical time for them to ply their trade when the end of school bell goes for the day. I knew I could survive now. The bullies were not as bold as I had erroneously thought they were! By the time the bell went at the end of the school day, my father was already waiting. There was no time for the trolls to even attempt their trade. I rushed to my father beaming.

"I came early today so there will be no time for anybody to bully you. I promise I will always be here before the bell goes from henceforth so that there will be no time for those naughty children to harass you after school."

I went home very happy.

Every day, my father would spare a few minutes asking me how school was and reinforcing how wonderfully made and intelligent I am before we started our academic exercises of school assignments and reading. He also kept his word and was always at school early to pick me up as soon as the closing bell went. What was more, he got me a fountain pen too. That was magical. Everyone wanted to be my friend and touch my shining new pen. No other person in the whole school had a fountain pen. Even when it got stolen twice, my father replaced it. He told me he expected anything perceived to be the tool for my new found confidence to be stolen and had got three just in case.

"My dear daughter," he said, "the pen is just a fringe benefit to reward you for being a good and hardworking child. Call it reinforcement tool if you wish. The key thing is for you to understand that your confidence lies within you. You are the one that decides and directs what can affect you, not those around you. Once you are able to do that, you become very secure in your own skin. The reason is simple; no one can ever steal what lies within you." My daddy said.

Gradually, I developed confidence and self-esteem the size of a cathedral. Something some persons would come to find repulsive and others would find attractive. More importantly, a trait I would come to love and utilise in negotiating my life journey. My father had given me a rock solid foundation that can never be eroded.

I am my father's daughter. I am unapologetic about it.

BUILDING ON THE ROCK SOLID FOUNDATION

I have a vivid recollection of how an aunt of mine came to visit us for a few days. She sent me to fetch her wallet on one occasion when she was going to send me on an errand. I got her the wallet and stood there waiting for her to give me the money. She opened the wallet, gave me some cash and sent me to buy her a few drinks down the road. I happily went on the errand. Thought nothing of the event and moved on.

A few days after she left, my father called me. "Sit down my daughter," he said. "I noticed the other day when your aunty opened her wallet before you, you were staring inside it."

"Why were you staring into a wallet that did not belong to you? Did you keep anything in there?"

I looked at my father in surprise. Little did I know that he was watching me on that day. I marvelled at the crisp Naira notes in my aunt's wallet when she opened it and I could not avert my gaze. The notes did to my eyes what a magnet would do to nails.

"I am sorry daddy but she opened it in front of me."

"That did not mean you had to burrow into the wallet and visually remove all the money therein with your eyes young woman," he replied. "You exhibited the attitude of a greedy person. Never look into a wallet, bag or box that does not belong to you. Even when they are opened in your presence, avert your gaze or out rightly turn your back. Never be snared by things that do not matter.

Those things are distractions. Instead, feed your mind from within and focus. Feasting on your distractions will starve your focus and trust me, you do not want that my dear Princess." I looked at my dad in amazement. I was glad for one thing though; he did not reprimand me in the presence of my aunty or anyone else for that matter. I remember how I took that discussion as gospel truth on the day, but came to gradually understand the proper implication of that conversation over the years.

He was teaching me the principles of self-worth and how not to be distracted by 'all that glitters which is not gold'. He was building daily on the foundation he had laid in me. I was humble enough to sit at the foot of this master and learn – even though sometimes, my learning was not voluntary.

By now, it must be apparent that I was raised by a man who taught me not to toot my horn and yet, he always told me 'to remember whose daughter I am!' That was a paradox that initially, as a child growing up, was difficult to comprehend. It was a challenge to reconcile the balance he was teaching me to acquire. Pa. Richard was one of those rare persons who are consistent in their actions and values. He lived what he preached so it was not difficult to learn from him by just being with him – that is, if one chose to learn. The reason I say this, is that learning, in my opinion, is a choice and it is lifelong. A person first has to unlearn certain things, to enable them re-learn how to learn new things.

Pa. Richard built my self-confidence daily. He ensured that I imbibed life enhancing principles and values as a child that some persons may never understand even in adulthood. I remember one occasion when a lovely car went past two of us and I turned around to have a better look at it. "Why are you straining your neck to the point of almost breaking it?" My Father asked.

"Daddy that was a lovely car that just went past us and I like it," I replied. "Did you not see it when it was approaching us Loretta?"

Oh no…not my full name now! That means another long lecture, I thought to myself. However, my meek response was "Yes, I saw it approaching us Daddy. It was so I could get a better look at it that made me turn my head when it eventually went past us."

"Turning your head to look at something you have already seen is symbolic; it tells me you yearn to have that thing. It signifies the fact that you have crossed an admiration boundary, into a want zone. It is often a tell-tale sign of greed."

I looked hard at my daddy and he held my gaze. Then I looked away and burst out angrily, "Daddy, but I am not greedy. I just admired a car I liked." "You are not greedy yet, but if I do not teach you now about the thin lines between admiration, need and greed, you will not know when you slip into greed."

"I do not understand you daddy. You tell me every day to aim high and go for what I want. I see a car I like, I look at it and now you complain that I am acting greedy?" "My dear daughter, when you saw the car, you liked it. That is okay. You mentally hold that picture in your mind's eye. Turning around to look at the car again and again will not get you the car. It is that mental picture you hold in your mind, which will propel you to work hard and achieve the things that will make you, get the car. Remember whose daughter you are. Remember your pedigree. Nothing, absolutely nothing material, should make an individual of your standing compromise your standards. You are born great my daughter. All you need is within you already and you need not be moved by material things. That car is beneath you. Why do you let it control you? To the extent you no more have control of your neck? You should control your environment at all times. Do not be moved by what you see, but rather be propelled by what is within you. You are in charge! You should keep the mental picture of the car and do the work to get you the car. You have acknowledged that straining your neck or even breaking it in the process will never get you that car. So why do you have to do it?"

"I am sorry daddy,' I said humbly. "I understand what you mean now." "Now, that is my daughter!" He replied with a broad grin. "Physical poverty is easy to correct my daughter. However, poverty of the mind and soul is something that mortgages men and women for eternity. It prevents their growth and the actualisation of their true potential. To truly actualise your calling in life, you must levitate above poverty of the mind and soul."

"So daddy, you will agree with me that it is not a crime to desire the car. What you are saying in essence is not to let the desire for the car becloud my judgment. The reason being that I will get all I wish for and more in due course with hard work, dedication and patience."

"I have never doubted your intelligence," he said, laughing, in that calm voice I miss so much.

"Alright daddy, I am not even old enough to drive yet," I said laughing. "I shall buy that car for you someday when I would have made enough money to get it. I completely understand now, I am born rich…. able to have all I need with time and of course 'all I want' as well." I said the last part of the sentence with a wink and my daddy laughed.
"I do not know about getting all you 'want' in life Taa," he laughed. "Loretta, the wants of humans never end you know?"

"Haha hha…I knew you would fall for the bait" I laughed, "I know that 'needs' are different from 'wants'. I however, will have many of my 'wants' actualised too and before you say anything further, let me reassure you, that they will all be good 'wants' Daddy." I said, grinning from ear to ear. My father smiled. He knew I had gotten a complete grasp of his lecture for the day.

The message sank in, never to leave me for all eternity. I was born great and greatness resides in me. Even if there were things I wanted, I understood that I would get them in due course. I would not compromise my values or be moved by materialism to descend to a level where I was being controlled by material things. My dad was equipping me for the days ahead and I dare say, he equipped me well as you will come to see later in the book. He was teaching me the basic tenets of delayed gratification and the joy of taking pride in the work of one's hands.

I am my father's daughter. I am unapologetic about it.

WHEN THE FLOWER BLOOMS IT IS BECAUSE THE PLANT IS BEING WATERED

I got admission on the merit list to do my secondary school education in one of the best schools at the time – Federal Government Girls' College Benin City (FEDIBEN). Looking back now, I am of the opinion that it was divinely programmed for me to attend the school. I could have gotten into any school of my choice because my entry scores were very good. However, Benin naturally was my first choice. I could not be too far from home. Going to boarding school as it were was already generating chaos in my household, so going outside Benin, was out of the cards completely.

My mother was not happy that her daughter was going to be put in a school where there would be "many enemies and children from homes she could not account for." I could not blame her at all. Considering my near psychologically wrecking experience with bullies in primary school and the paranoia of a woman married in a "serial monogamous setting", we can account for her thought pattern.

Pa. Richard on the other hand, was keen for me to go to the boarding house. "Go and learn how to relate with others," he said. "Go and learn how to navigate the full onslaught of the world. The only thing you must always remember is whose daughter you are." On my first day of resumption, we set out for the school like it was a funeral ceremony. I suddenly became very afraid and home sick at the prospect of leaving my parents and dear siblings.

My mummy on her part was crying and suggesting that I start as a day student first, then gradually be eased into the system and from the second year, become a boarder. My Father on the other hand was adamant. I was to go full blitz. I would start as a boarder and finish as a boarder.

No one spoke on that short drive from home to the school. When I saw the gate of the school, which would almost be my home for the next six years of my life, my heart sank! We got down from the car and I saw many other little girls looking as forlorn as I was. I saw many mothers crying and most of the men stood and looked around with that deceptively stoic look, while deep down, they must have been as anxious as the rest of us.

Then I saw the big girls! My God, then I thought they were big – they looked big. These senior girls in the school were on hand to welcome us, the new entrants and start our orientation. They looked like amazons. They reassured the parents and along with the staff, proceeded to check our boxes and rid us of every contraband material, which by the way was virtually everything in our boxes.

Amidst all the drama of resumption day, I was more fascinated by the senior students who were helping with the school entry process. I observed them and was particularly taken in by the majestic grace and confidence of one of them. She seemed to float above the rest. She had a presence I could not explain. She reassured my parents I would be fine. She introduced herself to my father as Miss II, the head girl of the school. There and then, with no knowledge of what the implications were, or of what being a head girl truly meant, I resolved that I had to become the head girl of the school before I left.

Miss II made being a head girl so attractive and effortlessly fulfilling that I just had to have it on my to-do-list. I told my daddy the newest addition on my to-do-list immediately I got a moment. Trust my father to back me a hundred per cent.

After the lengthy admission formalities, I bonded with another very lovely and soft-spoken young lady Miss OO who made my entry into FEDIBEN seamless. She reassured me, told me not to cry when my parents left and helped me arrange my belongings in my locker (wardrobe equivalent). when I got there and found many other young girls like me, stood, staring at their full buckets of water. The house prefect came and told us all in a no-nonsense voice to take off our clothes and do justice to the task of taking a bath.

Very shy, we each took off our clothes and had our bath. That was the beginning of the bonding experience. After that day, we got the message – life here was communal, just get on with it.

I had my bouts of homesickness. I sit back and smile today as I write, because I can just remember that unique smile Miss OO had. She literarily took my hand and mentored me. I remember how I used to lose the key to my locker where all our belongings were kept almost every other day. She helped me get the carpenter repeatedly to break and refashion the lock. It got to a stage; she tied my keys onto a key holder belt I had to keep around my waist.

FEDIBEN for me had the good, the bad and the ugly! However, I would not trade my experience in those six years for any other. Everyone was not as nice as Miss OO. There were the terrible senior girls who used to dish out servitude and act like they were princesses in castles. As the tiny new entrants to the school that year, we were at the bottom of the 'food chain'. The bigger 'sharks' had little mercy. I had to learn quickly to devise means that would enable me excel at my primary assignment which was to grow in learning and character.

I was her bunkmate: which means we shared one of the double-decker beds we had back then in school. I used to sleep on the top bunk. She took me to the dining hall that first evening where I met with the rest of my kind.

My first morning, when the giant "lorry tire rim" which was our school gong was sounded, I opened my eyes and saw her smiling. It was a cold morning. She told me to take my bucket of water outside to the place where we had our bath. I was shocked when I got there and found many other young girls like me, stood, staring at their full buckets of water. The house prefect came and told us all in a no-nonsense voice to take off our clothes and do justice to the task of taking a bath.

Very shy, we each took off our clothes and had our bath. That was the beginning of the bonding experience. After that day, we got the message – life here was communal, just get on with it.

I had my bouts of homesickness. I sit back and smile today as I write, because I can just remember that unique smile Miss OO had. She literarily took my hand and mentored me. I remember how I used to lose the key to my locker where all our belongings were kept almost every other day. She helped me get the carpenter repeatedly to break and refashion the lock. It got to a stage; she tied my keys onto a key holder belt I had to keep around my waist.

FEDIBEN for me had the good, the bad and the ugly! However, I would not trade my experience in those six years for any other. Everyone was not as nice as Miss OO. There were the terrible senior girls who used to dish out servitude and act like they were princesses in castles. As the tiny new entrants to the school that year, we were at the bottom of the 'food chain'. The bigger 'sharks' had little mercy. I had to learn quickly to devise means that would enable me excel at my primary assignment which was to grow in learning and character.

I worked hard academically. I put in the effort and I got results. I began to top my class. I did so well, that it was proposed I should be co-opted into the then "gifted school being set up in Suleja in Nigeria". I was to sit for the examination then, but my father disagreed with the concept; his argument was that if you removed all "the so-called gifted ones" from a group of students, who would stimulate the rest you left behind? A good mix was required in his opinion, to enable schools produce people who are at par with each other and not miles apart in excellence. However, a part of me, till this day, still think my daddy did not just want me to move away from Benin, too far away Suleja or maybe a bit of both. Either way, I ended up not joining the 'gifted ones' in Suleja.

"Spread your wings my daughter – spread them beyond the four walls of any school. You do not require any school to reinforce your 'giftedness' for it lives in you and you will take it way beyond our shores one of these days".

"Sure daddy,' I responded. "I shall spread it worldwide! Let's do a high-five to that." We were there 'High-fiving' with my mum and other siblings laughing in agreement.

I had a gift from a very young age, which my father had nurtured. It was the ability to read. Like you remember, he set me on the reading path from as early as 2-3 years of age. I read every author readable by the time I was in secondary school and every subject under the sun I could lay my hands on was fodder. The fall out of my reading became writing. I began writing essay competitions in secondary school and for each one I wrote, I won a Prize. Many of the Prizes required me to travel out of Benin officially to states where the presentation ceremonies were held. I often had a teacher with an official car for such trips.

Some of the perks of being in a Unity School as the Federal Government Colleges are called. My writing exposed me to the world. I was on stage every other term. My audiences began to grow as I won essay after essay competition.

As my laurels increased on all front, so did my 'haters'. Many of them did not even realise they were hating. However, they could not comprehend why one girl seemed to have it all. Was she the only one in the school? Definitely not! So why was she getting all the accolades? Looking back now, even I can empathise with their self-imposed dilemma.

On the home front, I noticed my father had begun fretting a bit about my literary twist. I wrote my first full book manuscript and handed it over to my father at the age of thirteen. He read it, and never said anything about it for many months. One day, I told him I was making a choice of subjects and that I had included literature in my selection. He looked at me and said, "If you continue like this, I fear you may abandon medicine, which you told me was your first career choice."

"Ah, daddy, you see, I have changed it already. I now want to become an architect when I grow up. I love all those buildings I see each time I travel. Besides, I think we need to develop our own environmentally relevant building materials and buildings. Like using 'baked earth' instead of cement for our buildings will maintain our house temperatures better".

My father looked at me, very surprised. "So when did this happen and I did not know?" He asked laughing.

"It is happening as we speak daddy," I laughed too.

"By the way daddy, where is the manuscript I gave you months ago?" Pa. Richard gave me the look…. "I see you want to be many things, an author too? Is that why you have picked literature?"

"Daddy, you know I love literature. You opened the door to the art for me. Why are you reluctant that I pursue it?"

"I want you to focus Loretta. I am beginning to see a trend towards deviation."

"And pray what am I deviating from? You tell me I can do anything I choose to do. No matter how many, now you tell me I am deviating?"

"Okay my dear daughter, I looked at your manuscript. I read the story. It was very good. I will look for how to put this out there once you finish your final secondary school examination"

"Daddy! That is still a good 3 years away at least!"

He smiled but said nothing.

For some strange reason, that was where my manuscript ended all those years ago. Pa. Richard tactically did not want me to pursue writing on a full scale. He must have been afraid that if I did that, I would not become a doctor.

This was one of the times I saw a flaw in my father manifest. It was the one time I think he put his selfish desire before what I wished for as a human being. I have completely forgiven him for it because I understand he did it out of love. He must have felt that if I pursued writing, I would not be able to combine it with the rigor of becoming a doctor. On the flip side, he may just have been wrong. However, none of us can ever control for that experiment anymore.

These days, I just think and say aloud to myself; "Well, daddy, I think you just helped reverse the order. So I can be doctor first and author thereafter not author first as I initially intended. At the end of the day, the order does not really matter". From my own experience with my father, and in today's modern world, I have learnt that if my child were to give me half a manuscript, I will help the child turn it into a full book irrespective of age or projected professional trajectory. I have realised from the strengths and weaknesses of my father – he was only human after all and he did some things that may have missed some marks.

Back to my school travails, I got more prizes at each prize-giving day with no sign of relenting. I kept churning out the essays and picking up the prizes that came with them as well. A situation that became directly proportional to the annoyance of some around me, causing seniors to bully me and contemporaries to whisper things not so nice behind me. I was prepared to deal with my travails. If you have paid attention in preceding chapters, you would know that my tool kit was air tight to deal with whatever I got thrown at me. Thanks to Pa. Richard.

One incident I went through in school, which was to change my life forever, was when I wrote a particular essay, where the top three prizes were to go the United States for twelve weeks on leadership training. I wrote and won the essay. I was congratulated in school and it was aired on the National Television that I was going abroad. I was excited - so were my parents and siblings. Then, for some strange reason, my name got swapped out of the list. Let us call it the 'Nigerian factor'. I was devastated. I went back home to my parents and told them I was done going to school. I was in my 4th year of secondary school going on the 5th. Trust my mother to come up with her 'enemies theory'.

"Is this how the enemies want to derail my daughter's education?" She wailed!

"This country is evil. How can they connive to take what belongs to this little girl? My God will surely ask them". Even through my tears, I could not help smiling feebly at my mother's tirade and the significance she gave to her enemies. It was the loopholes in accountability in our nation's system that cheated me out of what was rightly mine not necessarily her enemies. In another way, one could call those who perpetuated such loopholes and capitalised on them, the 'enemies of progress'. So overall, mummy was right even in her drama.

All this while, my father said nothing. However, his anger was palpably loud even in his silence. He told my siblings and my mother to let me be.

Two days later, he called me. I was very sad and low in mood. He told me to get my act together and put the injustice behind me.

"No daughter of mine will run away from any battle with her tail between her legs. You may have lost this war, but you have a battle out there to win my daughter. The battle of life! Tell me when you are ready to go back to school. For you will go back to school, you will hold your head high. You do know whose daughter you are?"

"Thank you daddy," I said, hugging my father. "I will go back to school next week – which is 2 days from now."

"That is my girl. Now go tell your mummy anything you want to eat and she will prepare it. Do you wish for Turkey? Chicken? Even Goat meat? Let me know and we shall fetch one for your mother to make us a delicacy" I smiled.

I need to let it out at this stage if I have not done so before now, that my daddy felt a good meal could cure all things. Well, I guess as the doting father he was, it was his way of pampering us.

So, it was, that I went back to school. I was not in a very good place at the beginning when I first went back. I had been given time formally off school and was just supposed to proceed to the next class when I came back. The then Minister for Education had seen to that. Since I did not travel any longer, I had to come back and tidy up my school work. This meant that I had missed some deadlines. Many of my teachers were very understanding and supportive.

However, one was not very nice to me. It was my Economics teacher. She got very upset that I was submitting the term project late. I tried to explain my recent aborted travelling plight, which by the way was no kept secret in the school. She screamed at me in the staff room to take it away that she would not accept my project because it was past the submission deadline.

Other teachers tried to explain to her but she would not listen. I drew myself to my full height, looked at her and said: "The next time you see me in your economics class, you can send your big fat dog to bite me." I smiled and walked away.

That was the last time I ever entered an Economics class in FEDIBEN. The teachers who were my friends tried to convince me to reverse my decision. They explained that I needed Economics as it was the only link I had between the pure science subjects which I had picked, and the social sciences should I decide to change my mind in terms of a future career. For me, there was no going back. I never went back to any economics class in FEDIBEN. However, I studied for the subject as a private student at GCE level and I made an A in it. Simply put, I knew whose daughter I was, and no one, absolutely no one, was going to talk down on me or call my bluff. Not then, not ever. This was one of the battles of life my father had spoken of and I was determined to win.

Many years later, I met my old Economics teacher Mrs O. I told her how badly she hurt me all those years ago. She very promptly apologised and asked that I forgive her actions. She explained she might have been going through an emotional turmoil at that moment in time. I told her I forgave her the very next day. However, I had promised myself on the day that I would definitely bring what I perceived as less than a professional attitude she displayed at the time to her attention again someday; no matter how long it took me. I was only telling her so she does not make a similar mistake again since she still taught in the school. She admitted I was right and today, we are good friends. We have a lot of love lost between us now. Some of her children are mentees of my husband and I. Life surely is a three hundred and sixty degrees wheel that is in constant motion. We all need to be careful what we sow today.

On the part of the senior students, my aborted trip was an impetus that galvanised them into proving a point to me. The point was that she who flies, will sometimes fall to the earth with a huge thud. When she falls, those who were not on her flight trajectory will be waiting to rub the fall in. I was punished with reckless abandon for the most flimsy things. It got so bad; some of my teachers came to the hostel once, when they did not see me in the class. I was serving some mundane punishment I rather not put in print. The teachers asked what I had done and told the senior girls to let me go.

They were just plain jealous. Their response shocked the teachers as much as it made me cringe. I have never forgotten it. They told the teachers "Yes, we are jealous! She is not the only one in this school. Please, let our jealousy be and let us be!" I write these incidents not because I am bitter about it. Far from it, I write them so that someone out there will understand how hot and lonely it can become at the top and be prepared for it. To remain at the top is harder than getting to the top. To pick up the pieces after a real or perceived fall is not an easy thing. However, it is something we have to learn. All we need to do is to be determined in the face of adversity to rise. It is not a crime to fall however, it is a crime to fall and stay fallen. I adopted this mind set. It gradually evolved that I began to look forward to being punished. That way, I just went through the motions mechanically and moved on. I knew that what had a beginning surely had an end as well. I patiently served my time without losing focus. I did not bother to tell my parents of the ordeals because I lost count of them.
I dealt with each on its merit and pushed them behind me as I forged on. I did not relent on excelling. Every punishment was another reason to excel. I still topped my class despite all the travails I had that year.

I look back and smile. I ended from FEDIBEN on the highest note ever. I was unanimously voted by the students to be the head girl of the school the next year. I will use this opportunity to thank all the students who many years ago, put their confidence in me to lead them. Especially, those who took the campaign upon them, that I must be made the head girl. I remember every single one of you with humility; words cannot describe my appreciation to you all.

There must have been something all of you saw in me, which made you all my enablers. Yes, your faith in my abilities made me keep a promise I made to myself on my first day in FEDIBEN …to become the head girl just like Miss II who had welcomed me to the school. I did my best to lead by example. I hardly gave corporal punishments. I got the job done with an excellent team of other prefects I was blessed to work with. I left FEDIBEN on an all-round high note – academically, a result with straight 'A's, character that was reinforced and solid as well as a gratitude to God that was boundless.

It was clear to me then that if you can visualise something, you can create it. Our destinies lie in our dreams and visions. The work to get things done is only fifty per cent of the whole. Having been made in the image and likeness of God, with free will, it means we can also like God, create what we choose. What we choose to build with the ability we have each been given remains our decision to make. When we dream it, all we need is faith as small as a mustard seed to call our vision into being. There is an old Japanese Proverb my father used to tell me often. In fact, there was a time he told me to write a one-page analysis of it before he got back home from wherever it was he went on the day. I did the assignment and gave Pa. Richard my one page write-up on his return. He read what I had written, looked at me and said with a smile, "Well done!" We discussed my write up and he explained the proverb even better to me. By now, you must be wondering what the proverb was. It is simple and straight to the point:

"Vision without action is a day dream; action without vision is a nightmare." Japanese Proverb

You can trust that after doing that exercise as a child; I have walked around with that proverb in my heart. The meaning continues to contribute to what propels me to reach for even greater heights – I am no fan of nightmares and simultaneously not a dreamer without strategic action. I dream it, I pray it and do it.

I am my fathers' daughter – both my earthly and heavenly fathers; and I am unapologetic about it.

HOW TO BE LEFT HANDED IN A RIGHT HANDED WORLD

It is in retrospection that I realise how blissful and truly formative growing up was for me. I had a father who would listen to me, empower me and reinforce in me, the fact that God fearfully and wonderfully created me. Daddy told me daily how I could be anything I wanted to be.

You see, my daddy was about 30 years older than my mother like I stated in the earlier chapters. He was better educated in 'terms of certificates' and greatly travelled. My mother on the flip side, was only a standard six holder, from a more humble background but 'a very intelligent woman' without the glory of 'many a paper certificates'. I am repeating this, to enable any reader have a better understanding of the gulf between these two people. This will enhance a better understanding of certain events I am soon to describe.

By virtue of the gap in their background, my mother's mantra was to discipline us physically using the 'by fire and by force method'. My Father on the flip side would discuss with you and explain very calmly, ensuring that you understood what and why you need to make recommended changes. The two had modus operandi that were the opposite of each other. Both ways, a balance arose that gave us the children, a combination of character and learning that was formidable. My father especially ensured we understood the meaning of internal validation and why we did not require external people to define and validate our existence.

I look back and cannot remember the one time my father hit me or ever shouted at me. However, my mother was a 'shouter' and the fact that my ears are still on either side of my head to this day, remains a miracle. My ears were my 'handles'. The two pieces of appendages that bore my entire body weight any time I erred. My mummy would lift my siblings and I up using our ears and then twist it while we were suspended mid-air.

You would think we would be very scared of my mother because of her punitive measures – but the truth was, we were not. We looked forward to her methods as our ears gradually became mutated to accommodate the pain. We feared my mother but the parent we truly respected was our father.

We used to joke among ourselves "mummy will only pull our ears and swing us from side to side. Then all will be well that ends well. However, daddy on the other hand, will preach daily till thy kingdom comes – the matter does not end. It became such a perpetual torment that we rather not upset the balance. We conformed, to only a flick of a glance from daddy but mummy had to shout the entire house down to get a response from us. We had deep respect for daddy and a 'superficial fear' for mummy.

I shall share with you dear readers, an event that exemplifies the difference I am trying to explain. Once upon a fine day, on a certain Nigerian street, my mum sent me to boil some yam to prepare pounded yam. I promptly went ahead to peel the yam and added some water to it in a pot. Then, I lit the cooker, set the pot on it so its content can boil. Next, I confidently added some salt to the yam for taste. When my mum asked me if I had put the yam on fire, to boil and make the pounded yam, I said, "Yes!" Then all of a sudden, she stopped in her tracks and from out of the blues, asked me "Did you put salt in the yam you are boiling?" "Yes mummy," I said. "I put some salt. But it will not be too salty as I tasted it and it was okay."

At this point, my mother had started shouting and calling on over ten generations of her ancestors to come and save her from me!

"Who puts salt in the yam boiled to make pounded yam?"

"God, you know I am doing a good job oo! A great task of ensuring this girl can cook so that she will find a good man that will marry her. Yet, just to boil yam to pound yam, she added salt? This pounded yam will turn out very bad. It will be like mashed potato without any stickiness."

I ran away knowing that this time, not only my ears were in trouble...

My daddy, who had been engrossed in whatever it was he was reading, heard my mother's screams! I am sure, that even the four corners of the earth must have heard her. Pa. Richard came to us and said in his calm but firm voice: "Please let my daughter be. I am not raising her to be a slave and cook for any man. Any man who wishes to eat pounded yam should please pound it himself and not think my daughter is a pounding machine. As for my meal today, I will have no pounded yam. I will just eat my boiled yam like that."

My mother retorted with a shrill scream, "If I do not train her well, they will laugh at me that I have failed. The enemies will laugh at me. God knows I have tried! Instead of the enemies to laugh at me, I will make sure I beat how to cook into this your big head! "My father came in between us and saved my head on the day. He told me to follow him to the living room. My mother's eyes were spitting lava but there was not much she could do - for when Pa. Richard spoke, all had to listen. Her inclusive!

When we got to the living room, my dad told me to sit down. Next he asked me if I understood why my mother was angry.

I responded that it was because I used salt in boiling yam meant for pounding.

"What does the salt do to the yam? And why should you not have added salt in it?" He asked.

"I do not know daddy. I do not know. Mummy never told me. She only just started shouting and calling on her ancestors to help!" I giggled. My father could not help laughing as he proceeded to explain to me, why I should never again put salt in yam meant for pounding. "You see, my daughter, your cooking salt, is sodium chloride isn't it? It is made up of ionic molecules that will break up the carbohydrate bonds in yam, thereby reducing the viscosity or binding force when you start to pound. The end result is that the pounded yam will not have the nice adhesive texture, which makes our meal stand out. Rather, it will be fluffy and may not even mix uniformly causing little lumps we call "seeds". You spend more energy pounding that kind of yam and despite that, the end product is less than satisfactory to the taste buds."

It was a eureka moment for me. Now I truly understood why I did not need to put salt in the yam for pounding ever again. Not that I was ever going to forget my mother's screams and call on her ancestors in my entire life time, but now I would not just act didactically without understanding the principles. "Thank you daddy," I said.

"You are welcome my daughter. The other thing I want you to understand is that even though you learn how to cook, you are not perfecting that skill because a man somewhere wants to eat. You are not perfecting that skill because it is your task to please one man. You will perfect your cooking skills because you need to make good healthy meals for your own self. If a man respects and pleases you in future, and you wish to express your acceptance of his good attitude by doing him the privilege of cooking him great meals, I have nothing against that. However, what I never want you to do is to think that your life revolves around getting married to a man. You are first and foremost, a human being with pedigree unparalleled. Remember whose daughter you are. Any man, worth his salt, will treasure and value you and that my daughter, will bring out the very loyal and loving best in you."

I looked at my daddy as he spoke. I was grateful then that he rescued me from my mother and he gave me an enlightening domestic chemistry lesson. Today, I look back and I am eternally indebted to him for liberating my mind from that aspect of society that throws people into boxes led by cohorts like my mother. I am glad he unleashed my wings, so I could fly.

Well, what I never told my mother all those years ago, is that I actually never really had deep respect for her. I had fear 'induced respect for her'. The type that after some time, fades away when one can no longer be bothered by the shouts, rants, ancestor summons and even the physical bashing. The type that if not properly handled could metamorphose into rebellion. I did not tell her how lucky she was to have my father who was a balancing act in our upbringing. I did not tell her how much I loved her for many years, because for a long time, I thought she did not love me. Now, some forty odd years down the line, I know better. My mother was a product of her environment and as such, she wanted to do the best to be the 'good mother' who raised the 'good daughters' that would in turn, perpetuate the 'goodness' of future female generations.

My mother found it difficult to be the left-handed person in a right-handed world. She also did not want us to become 'societal non-conformist' whereas my father actively raised us to be left-handed in a right-handed world. He wanted us to be unapologetically ourselves. He raised us to be accountable for actions. He raised us to be unafraid to become agents of 'societal change'.

In the entire quest to raise us as agents of societal change, my father still wanted that balance of us being societally grounded in our sociocultural heritage. He insisted that we do all communication in the home in Benin Language. He ensured that we had a good grasp of our cultural values – albeit, the positive ones. He reviewed our cultural heritage with us often and pointed out what he felt was not very good. He told us to discard such things and keep the positive aspect of our culture. It was my dad who first introduced to me, the concept of what I now call "cultural integration" as a way of uplifting societies. Cultural integration simply means taking what is great in one culture, and harmonising it with what is great in another, while discarding the negatives from both.

An example was how in the early days, many families did not see the need for girl child education or empowerment. However, this was not the way to go if we as a people wanted to progress. We need to educate our girl children and empower them. In the same way, we need to now raise our boys on how to deal with the empowered and educated crop of women coming up. This is because; they cannot do to these women, what their fathers did to their mothers without some serious consequences.

On the flip side, our cultural heritage is rich and brimming over with many positive attributes; the culture of respect for elders, the concept of taking care of our elderly and many more. I guess the Benin Prince in my father made him determined that we never for once lost sight of our roots. He used to say and I quote, "You have to know where you are coming from, for you to have a focus of where you are heading to."

I still have memories of the funny sight we must have cut – reading out Shakespeare in English language and then discussing the meaning of what was read in Benin language. Or when we would sit and analyse a Beethoven and Chopin piece in Benin language. There were those times when we ran into problems because there may not have been a ready equivalent Benin word for many things. None the less, we always found a way to create some phrases and get around things. Besides, we could just flip back to English when the challenge was too much.

What these sessions did for my siblings and I was that we all speak our native tongue perfectly. As I got older, I began to appreciate what my father had done for me. I am proud of my Benin heritage. We may have our challenges now as a people, but no one can deny our place in the history of the world order.

I am my father's daughter. I am unapologetic about it.

WHEN THE BUBBLE BURSTS

As at the time I was immersed in the growing up process, I thought the relationship I had with my parents, especially my daddy was the norm rather than an exception. I grew up believing that children had this kind of relationship with their fathers. How wrong I was, my bubble was about to burst.

In the interval between leaving secondary school and starting my University education, I had the freedom to visit friends in their homes. Something I could not do while in the boarding house all those years. It was on one of such visits that my bubble first met its needle. I came to realise that the average parent-child relationship in the society where I grew up was a far cry from mine.

I remember one particular event because it really upset me. I had gone to visit one of my good friends while I was in FEDIBEN and her father arrived from work. As soon as my friend and her two sisters heard their father honk the horn at the gate, they pulled me up from my seat and said, "run, follow us," I started running towards the front door because I thought they meant we should run out to welcome their dad. How wrong I was! They all looked at me with confusion on their faces and asked in unison, "where do you think you are going? We have to run into the room in the children's apartment from daddy. Instead you are running towards him? Is that what you do in your house?" They pulled me into the corridor that led to their rooms.

My dear readers, you cannot even begin to imagine my confusion!

Once we got into the room, I asked the girls, "So, who will welcome your father home?" All three girls looked at me and burst out laughing. "Welcome him home? No one does. Daddy likes to take a short rest once he gets back from work. He will spend some time in the living room and NN the domestic help will serve his meal; then he goes to his room and comes down when our mother gets back from work about two hours later. Then we all watch the national network news and spend
time together."

I pretended to understand them even though till today, I never have. When my father comes home from anywhere, we run straight to the gate, open it and jump on him as he gets out of the car. My siblings and I would struggle to snatch the bag of goodies he always had for us. Now as I think back, I find it difficult to remember a day my father left the house and came back in, without some basic goodies or snacks. It would range from Doughnuts and other pastries from the high-end corporative stores to roasted tropical delicacies like corn on cob or groundnuts from the roadside sellers. It did not matter which, there was always enough for us all to share. It was a tradition. We had to welcome daddy. As for mummy, we also had to welcome her entrance. However, expect no goodies and ensure all the housework had been done. In fact, it was almost like a taboo for either of my parents to come in, and we did not gravitate to their presence.

So you can imagine why I was upset by the drama at my friend's place. I was not angry, I was just wondering if this was the norm in other homes or if mine was the norm in other homes. When I got home, I recounted my experience to my parents and siblings. We all had a good laugh and my mother said, "Do you think everyone spoils children the way your father spoils all of you?

Anyway, as for me, whenever I come into this house you all must report immediately at the door. I must see my children quickly so I can be happy you are all in one piece." Pa. Richard laughed and said "our mummy only wants us to report on her arrival so she can be reassured all is well with us? That is so caring. We did not know you worry over us all this much." At this, everyone laughed.

My dad said to us "If you want to miss your goody bag, then do not come for a hug when I get back to the house."

"Nooo our goody bags must be actualised. Get ready to be hugged on arrival for a life time," we all responded.

"You see my dear children, every family has what works for them. Do not be alarmed when you meet other people and they do not live like us. What works for them is different. That is what makes society unique. However, for you to be unique in society, you must maintain those values that promote our shared humanity – those everyday things that money and position cannot buy, make you stand out.
Treat anyone around you with dignity and respect irrespective of class or creed. Always value yourself and understand your self-esteem without being proud."

The story did not differ much when I visited more friends. I finally gained insight that my family and upbringing was the odd one out. I was raised in a bubble – a bubble now burst. The good thing however, was that the foundation was so strong that it did not matter if the bubble bursted anymore. Some people had definitely done their part well – I am indebted to my parents.

I am my parents' daughter – and I am unapologetic about it.

GROWING UP EARLY

In 1997, my father died. My world collapsed. I was a third year medical student when my daddy passed on, to the great beyond. When Pa. Richard died, many persons came out of the woods and crevices, claiming to be family. He had opted for cremation and a Rosicrucian burial, which annoyed his family especially his maternal Benin Royal Family who could not understand how or why a son of theirs wished to be burnt.

Though traditionally the paternal kinsmen and women are in charge of an individual's burial rights, the maternal side agitated more against the cremation concept. In the end, he had the Rosicrucian burial but was not cremated. Many came out of curiosity to see a Rosicrucian burial, which was all done in the open. Pa. Richard made a grand exit from this earth plane.

After my father's funeral, a loud silence descended on us. We were young. My poor mother was devastated. In the twilight days, my dad was chronically unwell and resources had been grossly depleted. Some persons Pa. Richard officially entrusted the business of ensuring we did not lack financially after he died were more pre-occupied with their personal agenda than executing the wishes of a dying old man for the vulnerable family he left behind. So, I had no other option than to grow up fast. The responsibility of my schooling and that of my siblings fell squarely on my shoulders. The petty trading my mother engaged in at the local market did not amount to anything.

Relatives who had promised heaven and earth before my father died went AWOL. Friends vanished into thin air. It is easier to deal with lack if one has always lived in want. However, to have been raised in affluence and then, all of a sudden have it all swiped from under your feet is a more difficult scenario. It is psychologically demoralising and can redefine one's values. I think my father knew that such days might come which was why he ensured with every fibre of his being that he imbibed in us, the values he did.

It was all that grounding that kept me afloat and enabled me to make tough and difficult choices without thinking twice. There were many of such instances, which I cannot mention without talking about some key actors and actresses that have featured in my life journey.

Three of my father's friends deserve mention. The first two are Mr. OTY and Mr. PE. Both men took time out of their busy lives and sacrificed money from their own over budgeted purses to make some basic needs available for us. Then there was Mr O. He was there every Christmas for about ten years after my father passed on. He consistently ensured we did not lack what to celebrate the various festive periods with. Ironically, these three men were not the 'perceived closest' to my father when he was alive. There were others who we thought were his close friends and had expectations of. Those were nowhere to be found. Only these three came forth. These experiences thought me to have no expectations from others but rather, to realise that our helpers could be the least expected persons. I learnt that helpers come and go and while some may remain with us, many are in transit.

Adopting this mind-set has enabled me to maintain many relationships with people that may otherwise have gone sour because I am hardly disappointed by anyone since my default mode is very little expectation.

From the crop of the unexpected helpers, emerged an old school mate's father who I will call CA. He took on the task of seeking out a scholarship for me to enable me complete medical school. He went from pillar to post. Not relenting. There is no perfect human. He has his human flaws but I have learnt to overlook the flaws of men and women while holding on to their good attributes. CA took my plight to every prominent person within his social radar. One incident I remember vividly was when he took me to one of the few successful businesswomen in Benin City.

She listened carefully to how I was about to be thrown out of medical school for lack of finances to pay my fees. She took one long look at me and asked in a cynical voice that was laced with disdain "Do you not know what girls your age do to make money? Go and do just that my dear."

I took a long look at her again. I empathised with how much her inner ugliness engulfed her being. With pity in my voice, I told her "thank you Madam". No daughter of Pa. Richard Ogboro was going to descend to the level of having a conversation of this nature with this woman who clearly had skewed values. Not even if it meant physically starving to death - for my mind and soul were neither poor nor hungry.

I got up and walked out. Not angry, not sad, but very determined that in my life journey, no woman would come to me with her issues and go away without me attempting to find a solution.

CA, my friend's father, looked at her, shocked as I walked out, he could not believe his ears. I on the other hand, did not look back.

FO was another man who came on to the scene in the most unlikely circumstance. My big sister was unwell and was admitted under his care. As is customary in the medical profession, the boss does not need to be on the shop floor always. So his team took on the management of my sister's case. It transpired that certain medications required for my sister's care could only be purchased at the time from his private facility. When my sister was told the

60

price of one tablet and informed that she needed six tablets in total, she started weeping because she could not afford it.

I came and met her crying, and after she explained what the matter was, I told her to stop crying having assured her that I would get her medications. She asked me how and I told her not to worry. The truth was that I did not know how, but I knew one thing for sure and it was that I was going to get the drugs. The how would be sorted by God, after all, he is my heavenly father and I his special unapologetically trusting daughter.

I asked the doctors on the ward the directions to the boss and where I could purchase the medications. It turned out that at that time of the evening, FO was at his private facility. I found my way there and asked to purchase the drugs – six tablets in total.

The price was way out of my lean student budget as what I had could only cover three tablets. So I asked to see the boss. The nurses looked at me in consternation. I will not forget those two ladies who would in later years become great friends with me.

"He is busy with his private patients," they said.

"I will wait," was my simple response.

I waited. After about thirty minutes, I was ushered into the presence of one of the most imposing personalities I would ever meet. There was a large receiving space and one had to walk from the door to where he sat. He was with another younger man who bore some physical semblance to him. I walked right up to the two said good evening and then turned to FO. "My big sister is your patient. Your name hangs over her head in the hospital ward. We have been asked to get six tablets of the required medications and unfortunately, at this point in time, I am purchasing this drug for my sister who has no money. I only have the money that will cover three of these tablets at the current price. So, what you are going to do for us is to kindly save her life. The way you will do that is to very kindly give me all the six prescribed tablets for the price of three. If I had the money I would pay at the usual price. I do not have the money and my sister cannot die. Furthermore, if you think about it, the 'perceived monetary loss you make now' will not kill you and you would have saved another life. Remember, it is your name that hangs over her head."

FO looked at me all the while I spoke. I had intentionally adopted the approach of making my case heard without any interruptions as soon as I walked in. I stood there; waiting and looking at him with two defiantly flashing big brown eyes that meant business. Inside of me, I was tired and broken and silently said a prayer that God touch the heart of this man. I told myself that if he refused the appeal I would tell him I will sit in front of his door for as long as it took him to decide he was going to save my sister.

His voice brought me back to the present. "I said what level are you? I was told you are a medical student."

"The three hundred level pre-clinical class," I said.

"That is why I have not met you yet then." He turned to the man who sat next to him and said, "Call me the nurse."
When the nurse came, he instructed her to give me the six tablets for the price of three – half the total price.

The smile on my face must have lit up the room. I thanked him and made to leave his presence.

"I will see you in clinics," he said.

"You sure will, in about three months." I replied.

When I walked up to my sister's bedside, she started crying. Saying the situation was very bad. Then I told her I had got all six tablets and had handed them over to the nurses on the ward. They had already sent for her doctors (to come and prescribe the drugs on the ward drug card) so it could be administered to her.

My sister wept a bucket! Asking me how I got the money to buy the tablets – all six for that matter. I told her she needed to get her faith into action. All she needed was just a mustard seed size dose of faith!!

My sister did not die. FO and his team saved her. It was a most unlikely meeting for the man who would become one of my most inspiring mentors and friend. His job was to motivate me without him even understanding to what extent. It was a sure thing that we both looked out for each other three months after our initial encounter during my clinical posting; for both of us had made an impression on each other.

In my association with FO, I learnt many things. He reinforced the principles of hard work and determination my dad had instilled in me. An ambitious man, who would let nothing stand in the way of any of his goals, he further instilled in me how not to be content with a level of achievement but to keep aiming for new heights. His desire for excellence, mastery of keeping important communication lines open and seeking new ways of doing things was a good infection for me.

FO like most of my helpers along my life journey had one attribute I did not and still do not connect with. His, was an impatient streak with all things 'he perceived' slow or not inspiring. To some extent one can even justify this attribute in him, when you think of the results it may be generating.

However, I am of the opinion that sometimes, it limits his ability to notice what lies beneath and it underplays the human element, which I have come to know resides beneath all that 'tornado personality'. None the less, there is no perfect person. Not even my beloved Pa. Richard was perfect, so even though FO and I often have our differences, which I have never hesitated to let him know, we have over the years come to appreciate the greatness in each other.

No one can be around a personality like FO and not pick up one life advancing trait or the other. I picked up many. Most via what I term 'indirect mentoring' as the impatient streak does not make him the best of direct mentors. However, truth be told, I find that indirect mentoring builds a more determined individual. All you have to do as a mentor is live by example or give a little direction and the mentee runs actively with it.

Significantly, FO played a great role in me eventually leaving the shores of Nigeria for further training abroad. He did a lot more than he actually knows himself and for his assistance by error of commission or omission, I am eternally grateful with a loyalty I cannot even dilute no matter how much I tried because I was raised by a father who drummed the value of saying the truth (no matter how bitter it may be perceived by me and or the receiver) and consistency of purpose into me.

I am my father's daughter. I am unapologetic about it.

SURVIVING SOCIETAL STEREOTYPES

After my father died, a lot of water went under the bridge. I cannot over emphasise how tough those times were. Just thinking about it brings tears to my eyes. There were times we did not even know when the next meal as a family was going to come from. We were used to a particular life style and adapting to the new hardship took its toll on each of us in many different ways.

Each time I reminisce on those times, I find that in the wake of all that physical hardship, what helped me survive and make the right choices then, was my lack of 'poverty of the soul'. In fact, the wealth of self- pride embellished by self-esteem that was infused into me by Pa. Richard, did not allow for poverty of any kind to tarnish my sense of self-worth. I never forgot for once and I never will forget, "whose daughter I am."

The period of hardship coincided with the time a new societal rave was eating deep into the heart of my people. Young women from my state of origin were leaving the shores of Nigeria in the wake of poverty to become prostitutes abroad. Some were innocent victims deceived into such trips but many too, were aware of the implications of such trips. However, they must have felt there was nothing else they could do. The societal cankerworm was flourishing and I was not insulated from it anymore.

Many of my mother's friends were the vehicles that drove this menace into our reality. I will never forget the way many of them came to our house like preys, to tell my mother how these beautiful daughters she has can change her life if only they travelled to the land of 'milk and honey' – Italy. They often said that because of the love and allegiance they owed my mum, they would foot the travel expense bills for my siblings and I. Now, it is important to note that these were people my mother grew up with. Many of them were apparently 'successful by their own yard sticks' having to Italy and returned to build what they considered beautiful houses and drive fancy cars. While my father was alive, they steered clear of my mother and some even laughed at her for marrying an old man. Therefore, when Pa. Richard died, for them it was a restricting wall that had collapsed and they had to make use of their perceived opportunity - they came in their droves to offer condolences and help us, so they said, but we knew the true reason why they flocked around.

What was worse? Our society turned a blind eye to the emergent evil and welcomed the ill-gotten wealth of these people with open arms. So much so that young girls were withdrawn from schools and packaged by human traffickers to 'fend' for their families back home.

I understand how poverty can push people to do whatever they can to make ends meet. I have been there so I can relate with the push and pull factors. I do not judge those who take the line of easiest resistance at all in life. My reason for this is because from my own experiences, I have come to know that the ability to be 'left handed in a right handed world' is no mean feat. It requires a rock solid foundation that is impermeable to the weathering harsh conditions and difficult situations we each experience in our life journeys.

Pa. Richard helped build what he could of the foundation that was my mind and soul. The rest was for me to either continue building on, or to demolish by the choices I made. I chose to build. I continued to read. I encountered many great men and women through their books. I actively sought and found knowledge in addition to that which I had the good fortune to having been born into. I deviated there, to reinforce the persona I had become so you can understand exactly why I am who I am. So, back to my mother's 'very helpful' friends.

There was a day one came to the house and was talking to my mother about the best way to escape this hardship we now found ourselves in. She pointed at me and said in our local language "What is this girl doing here now? She is just wasting away in the name of this school thing. Not that you even have money to pay the fees because she is always with you in the market. Do you know how much her mates are making in Italy? Look, you remember XYZ our friend that used to live near us while we were growing up?" My mother answered in the affirmative; "Yes, I do remember her and what about her? She drove past me the other day on my way to the market."
"Oh ho oo!"...her friend replied. "You see, I ensured her two daughters left for Italy two years ago when their father died. It is the older one who sent that car she now drives. The younger one is building a new house for her."

From where I stood, I could see the confusion, gradually beginning to creep into my poor mother's mind. Her eyes mirrored it. I smiled to myself and went about my duties, leaving my mother to the agent of societal brain washing that had paid her a visit.

There were the other group of helpers, who felt their male relatives that live abroad were 'God's gifts to women'. These ones came in their hordes. Telling my mother how they had one brother in the UK, USA, Canada, Russia or even planet Mars and how once my sisters or myself married their relative, our life would never be the same again. I remember one such 'come and marry my brother' tooting friend of my mother called Madam B. She came visiting on one of her trips to convince my mother that her brother was the reason I was born.

"I do not understand how someone will be packing women who will end up in husband houses in school and seeking money to train them."

My mother sat there, staring into space.

"My brother has been in Holland now for ten years. If your daughter marries my brother, he will ensure he takes care of you all."

I sat there, looking at her as she spoke with my by now hallmark 'look of pity'. I was sorry for her lack of insight. There is no harm in looking for a wife, a good one at that for one's brother. What was wrong in my opinion was the 'lack of value this lady had for human life.' If she had value for human life, she would understand that when you educate a girl child, you educate the nation. She would even push for her brother to marry an educated woman. She would not come here always trying to convince my mother to marry me off to her brother. A man I had never seen. A man I did not know what he did for a living. She always came armed with pictures of her brother taken against the background of fancy houses and cars she claimed belonged to him.

"Why are you looking at me like that?" Madam B asked me.
"I was just thinking about your offer Madam B. I was wondering why your brother has not found a wife for himself all these years."

"He did not want to marry an 'oyinbo' lady (meaning a white lady)."

"But I thought you said last time, that he had a child from a white lady over there."

"Oh yes," answered Madam B. "That was the woman he married just to enable him get his stay papers and become a citizen."

"So Madam B, you do not think a woman needs to be educated?"
"What is the use? When you will end up in one man's kitchen?"
Asked Madam B.

I smiled and walked away, shaking my head. There was no need to trade words with this lady at all. She was a product of her environment and a representation of the average mind.

The hard times got worse for us and it was not long before my mother tried to persuade me to go along with the evil suggestion of her friends. "My daughter, why not consider marrying one of these men? At least, the last one who came by himself from the United States had said he would marry you, leave you here to complete medical school, and once you are done, he would ensure you come to America to live with him. That way, he will pay all your school fees. That way, we would not have to worry where the next meal will come from."

I looked at my mum, I did not say anything. I just listened.

"Besides, by the time you graduate as a doctor, many men will start to run away from you. Once a woman is too educated, she begins to lack suitors. No man wants to marry a woman who will come and cover the pot of soup with her certificate!" My mother explained her face full of anxiety.

I laughed and said to her "Mummy, I cannot believe we are still on this matter. I thought daddy had often said there was even no need for me to bother to marry. He may have been right. That way, I get to cover my own pot with whatever I choose; not bother with another person's pot."
My mother smiled and answered, "Your father was a great man. But sometimes, I feel inside of me, that he was the only one who used to think the way he did. Because in the real world, things are not as he thought."

"It depends on where in the world your reality lies and where you are looking mummy." I laughed. "Never look for an elephant in the midst of cockroaches; mummy," We both burst out laughing.

I knew the day would come as the offers increased from every corner, when my poor mother would start to cave in. I could see my mummy's defences weakened daily as the noose of the hardship tightened without any escape route in sight. It took a discerning mind and a soul devoid of the concept of 'instant gratification' to see beyond those challenges and understand that perseverance and determination for my siblings and I to complete our education was the only tool of liberation required.

That day, I told my mother that she needed to remember whose wife she once was. I told her that the mere fact a pond is dry in the dry season does not stop it from still being called a pond. My father had imbibed in us, many principles to guide and guard our path. This was the time to draw on all that strength from within.

"There is no way mummy, I am ever going to do any of those thing your friends are suggesting. Tell them I said so. Tell them the reason is because I know whose daughter I am – I have got pedigree unlimited and so have you."

My mother looked at me with renewed hope in her eyes and answered "You are very right my daughter."

So a few days after that when yet another of my mother's relatives whose job was to recruit young girls for Italy came to our house on her 'mission to help', my mother had an argument with her.

"I think you should tell her by yourself," my mother screamed at Madam Eko as we used to call her. "Just let her hear it from you."

I walked into the living room to ask what the matter was. Madam Eko took the liberty to tell me herself what her mission was. She told me to sit down. Then she asked me: "Are you happy seeing your mother and siblings suffer like this?" "We are not suffering

Madam Eko." I replied. "We are just morphing through a different phase of life from what we were used to and it will come to pass," I replied.

"I asked you simple question, you are speaking big big grammar for me," she screamed. "This is the problem you have," she continued. "Instead of you to go out there and make money like all your mates are doing for their families, you sit here and suffer, speaking grammar and saying you are going to school."

She hissed long and hard. Stood up to her full intimidating height which was clad in one of the exotic laces of the time and multiple gold accessories whose total weight I thought to myself, would aid her quick obedience to the law of gravity and help drown her, were she toppled into a large body of water.

"Meanwhile, all the University girls I know are loose women. Hoping from one lecturer's bed or one big politician's bed to another. Instead of doing this thing on a small scale and earning useless Naira, why not just go to Italy and get paid in foreign currency? Swear you are not following some poor yeye (good for nothing) small boy about that campus and wasting what lies between your legs for next to nothing" she screamed at me.

You see, unlike the others, this was my mother's relative and so culturally, Mama Eko could not just be walked out of our house like the others before her. She also understood that loophole and she exploited it. She rained abuses on me but I refused to get angry. "Then send your own daughters, I said to her unflustered by her screams." My mother looked at me, worried, signalling that I keep quiet.

"They have all gone," she replied. I sent them to the oyinbo (white man) connections I made when I was in Torino. All these gold I have on, who do you think got them for me? My two daughters are doing very well there."

"Did my mother come to beg you for money or for food?" I asked her." Because, I cannot remember any of us, asking you to come here to start crying more than the bereaved."

She took one long look at me and shook her head sadly. "Time will tell, time will tell. At least, God can see I tried my best to help you people."

I could not help laughing, "God will understand Aunty Eko. God will understand that you tried and he will surely reward you for your efforts"

After that day, any one of these helpers who called when I was at home got the full weight of my diplomatic tongue. I was not going to just sit down and keep mute, giving audacity to incompetent thinkers to invade my personal space. Pa. Richard did not raise me that way. I was going to interrogate them and question their mission and vision like I had been empowered to do by my father. I was determined to expose to their minds, their own sycophancy – at least for those who had a shred of insight left.

The reason many of them called to 'render this so called help' was twofold. One was greed. They saw us as money-spinning tools that once trafficked would fetch them regular earnings. Secondly, when a group of people are down, they look for others to drag down into the pit with them. Why should it appear as though we were standing head and shoulders above them, on some sort of moral pedestal when we could all frolic in the mud together? So, they make the mud look like it is the most attractive place in the world, just to lure one into the mud with them. Deep in their hearts, even they are unhappy with their actions and seek companionship in their negative plight.

At such moments I blessed my father for the way he raised me. He brought me up not to think my life revolved around what I could get, but rather, what I could give my generation. Since I understood this, it was clear that the only way I can give was to first empower myself. A holistic education was key to my empowerment – not just getting paper certificates and he had set that 'holistic education in motion in his lifetime'.

So, all of my mother's friends, relatives and well-wishers hounding me with their 'help packages' were never going to get their way because I was determined to empower myself. My life would never be centred round materialism or instant gratification. I was never going to hinge my success in life on what lies between my legs. For goodness sake, I had a brain to figure out a life for myself and be productive. The reason was simple. It was from the words of my father – I am first and foremost, a human being with pedigree unparalleled and self-worth unequalled. Every day, I remembered and still remember whose daughter I am and no societal stereotypes can rein me in.

I am my father's daughter. I am unapologetic about it.

MEDICAL SCHOOL EXPERIENCE

I am giving special mention to my time in medical school in this chapter. The reason being because, it spanned a difficult yet unique period of my life. It will be difficult to set out every single detail of all that happened in my university days. The reason is not because I do not remember, but because, the narrative from just my university years alone can be two books by itself.

Spinets of my experiences in my university days have already sipped out in earlier pages. Nonetheless, there are some specific experiences which I consider must-be-told to enable the reader not only understand, but to also connect with why I place so much value on the grooming of the mind and the values my father imbibed within me.

While my classmates focused on their studies in the university, a greater part of my university days was spent fending for siblings and myself. When born with silver spoon and raised with a silver spoon, there is not much one can do, to change the silver look. I have always said feed children the way you wish them to look, and when they grow, the look will not depart from them. It does not matter what life throws at them later, they will still look the 'silver spoon part' -whether they will retain the values imbibed in them is another matter altogether. The reason I came up with these opinion is not hearsay, but rather, a product of my own life experiences thus far.

Even before my dad passed on, his chronic ill health had crippled our finances. Being the stoic personality he was, when I gained admission to the University, he sold some of his property to generate my school fees. I told my mum one-day, that despite the love I have (even though he is dead, I still love Pa. Richard) for my father, it did not stop me from understanding that marrying an older man with a previous family was like 'picking up the orange peel after someone else had sucked up the entire juice content.'

It may have its advantages on other fronts, but overall, it can be a difficult scenario. My daddy often expressed his sadness that he was unwell in later years and not able to do for us, what 'he perceived' he had done for our elder half siblings. I use the phrase 'he perceived' here because my half siblings in question, may not agree with Pa. Richard's opinion. I often reassured him that he definitely had more time to spend with us as a retired old man rather than a busy young or middle-aged man hustling on the ladder of life. That time spent was for me more important, than anything else in the world.

Despite my reassuring words, my father and I knew that I was not one to delude herself. I could see the burden my mother bore; one of caring for a loved one with chronic illness. I happily shared the burden with my mum without a second thought. Even when my choice of university location affected my career choice, I did not mind. I gave up becoming an architect because I wanted to go to a school near home so I could keep an eye on my father's care. I have no regrets at all becoming a doctor for two reasons. First, I am a doctor with a difference and not your regular breed and the second is because I know I can be anything I decide to be and do it well - I can be many things rolled into one.

Being a doctor does not stop me from doing many other things. These things apply to all of us, but the differences emerge from how we apply our selves.

So, in my university years I knew I had to learn how to fend for my life. It was clear I had to use my acquired tools to navigate this new harsh terrain. The realisation became even more real when daddy passed on in my third year. Things got really rough. I was about to be sent out of school at some point. In my mind, I resolved in the face of all the challenges that I had two options. The first was to complete my studies and the second was to complete my studies - I had to find a way somehow.

CA, my friend's father and the previously mentioned persons helped in their different ways. However, it was CA who eventually managed to secure me a scholarship. He pleaded my case to one of the Local Government Chairperson at the time who was gracious and magnanimous enough to grant me a scholarship for the rest of my 3 years in school. According to my benefactor, even though I was from another local government area originally he would award the scholarship because when Edo girls drop out of school and engage in prostitution at home
or abroad, no one asks for or is concerned about their local government area of origin. They are all classed as 'Edo girls'. This was a very humanist way to justify him giving me the scholarship and I will be forever grateful to him.

This man and his value for human life impressed me. His decision to award the scholarship came in the nick of time and saved my education. My mother was over joyed and my siblings elated. All of us went as a family to say thank you to this unique man. CA was at last fulfilled that he had managed to solve the burden of financing my education. He too, was thankful to this exemplary man.

Trouble broke in paradise when in my final year, after the payment of my scholarship, my benefactor invited me to his office. I went there as scheduled and he said he was due to go for an event in Benin City. He explained it was a conference which he wanted me to attend along with him so his contribution to helping humanity can be attested to by me. I had nothing to fear after all I knew this man well. The usual paraphernalia that is Nigerian

Government official convoy left the local government headquarters office on the outskirts of the state for the capital city, Benin. About an hour and half after, we drove into a huge compound and I realised that some of the convoy had vanished into thin air on the way. We alighted from the car and I got ushered into a lovely building. There was no conference going on. I had no clue where we were.

My host took me to a huge beautifully furnished reception room. Cooks and waiters emerged from the shadows and the huge dining table was laid with an array of lovely dishes. As we made to sit at the table, I asked my host why we did not go straight to the conference centre. To enable us eat he explained.

At that point, I knew something was amiss. I simply just sat there looking all pretty, cool, calm and collected, despite my head preparing for this battle I knew was about to rear its head in the war of my life.

After the meal, my host and benefactor said he wanted to speak to me in more conducive environs. We went to a smaller living room as opulent as the first. I liked the way he went straight to the point. Without mincing words he said he had seen me through school and I was almost rounding up. He explained to me how he felt it was better to go outside the country and do a sub - specialty training there. I concurred with his suggestions.

He asked where I wished to go and I said I had not thought about that. He replied that whichever country I chose to study, Canada, America or the United Kingdom, he would see to it that I get settled properly. He pointed to a bag in the living room locally called the 'Ghana-must-go-bag' in Nigeria. It was an average sized one. He asked me to look inside. I did. What I saw inside the bag was very attractive. It was loaded with crisp Naira notes. That was to show me how serious he was about me. All the money therein was mine. I thanked him very nicely. My father did not raise me to be rude even though he raised me to have an opinion. More so, I

79

could not even have been rude to my benefactor even if I tried because my father had also taught me the meaning of loyalty. Loyalty that tells the truth directly to the person in question – questioning them directly if it was worth maintaining the loyalty.

I asked him why he was so kind to me. He saved both of us any hassle by saying in a very sincere tone that he liked me. All I had to do was sleep with him and all the offers would remain mine. I expressed my gratitude to him and explained to him very nicely that even though I was indebted to his good nature, I was not ready for the new direction his terms of engagement had taken. I zipped back the bag loaded with cash, stood up and asked that I be let out. His eyes blazed fire while mine reflected determination. He let out a sigh, brought out some white powder from his pocket, snorted some and asked me to explain why I was rejecting his offer. Was he not handsome? Was it not enough to buy me? "What is your price?" he asked.

"I must confess your offer is very tempting and you are a handsome man. I really hate to break your good heart and appear ungrateful. I have thought carefully about your proposal. I do not need it. I may want it, but I DO NOT NEED it. My needs are simple and you graciously met them all these years. However, I have very few wants and right now, my wants do not include your offer. So please, let me go and let someone else benefit from this offer. There are many out there who want this offer." I went down on my knees begging; appealing to the last glimmer of good within his inner man that I knew was there somewhere, submerged beneath the madness of lust that was engulfing him. He looked at me long and hard. Then told me to get up. He pressed a bell and one of the waiters appeared. He told the waiter to see me out. I left without looking back.

I came out of the gate: I did not know where I was. I looked around me and saw no loiters. All the houses radiated opulence with fences that could compete with the Biblical tower of babel. I randomly took a left turn and walked on as I wept. I wept not because I was angry, but because I was sad. I was sad because someone I had come to trust just slaughtered my trust on the altar of selfish desire. I was sad because I saw a good man give in to his inner raging demons. I was sad because I had come face to face with how our society rolls. Despite all of this, I was still grateful to this man. I only just wished he were able to exercise a bit more discipline.

As I walked on, blinded by my tears, a discussion I had with my dad many years before came into my mind. He told me how one needs to conquer self, to enable one make choices devoid of greed, selfishness and instant gratification. "To conquer self is no easy task. It requires a level of self-discipline and long-suffering to achieve – but in the end my daughter, it is what makes humanity evolve for good." The choice was hard. The offer was tempting. I would never crucify anyone, were they to take that offer. I also thank the man for letting me out without a struggle. Indeed there is still some goodness in everyone. However, I somehow knew that the choice was mine to make and that his offer was not for me.

I am my fathers' daughter. I am unapologetic about it.

MEDICAL SCHOOL EXPOSURE

Medical school exposed me to many more men like my benefactor. Many of them were my lecturers. They came in different shapes and sizes. Some were kind even in the demand for sex, others were vain and a few were plain evil. I was kind to all and I still am. I simply said 'my no' very nicely and many eventually became good friends over time. There were a few evil ones that required extreme measures, which I did not hesitate to dish out once I was certain their mission was one that could cost me my progress. The Paediatric department in my clinical medical school days was especially notorious as was Chemistry and Biochemistry in my pre-clinicals.

You see, for me, I have no problem if two mutually consenting adults decide to do whatever they wish with themselves. What I can neither comprehend nor accept is when lecturers use their power gradient to harass a student and then fail the student for saying no. I had such a malignant situation in Paediatrics with some of the lecturers and I had to use one of their kind to get them to let me be.

I spoke to the 'big boss in this organised ring of sex demanding lecturers. He was also one who had asked me for a sexual relationship. However, he was not malignant to me for some reason I still cannot understand till date because he made life hell for some before and after me. I explained to him that I was not ready to sleep with anyone in Paediatrics. He was quite pissed that those beneath his elevated position in the university wanted what he wanted. I knew his ego would set in. I worked unapologetically on it and in the end; he gave me a note to one of his friends in the department.

I became a case of 'touch not my anointed and do my prophet no harm'. The man who received the note said to me "So Prof is dating you?" My response was a knowing smile. At the same moment, Prof called on his internal office line (he knew I was there at the time). Both men spoke on the phone and the Professor confirmed he had sent me with the note. After the call, the man in front of me sighed and said to me:

"If Prof is already occupying your binding site, no one else should dare come in there."

I looked at him and smiled "Thank you Sir, for taking care of me. I will let Professor know of your good work."

Indeed I told the Professor about the magic of his note and call when we met later. He laughed and said to me, "There is honour among thieves my dear and you, young woman are one hell of a smart lady. Now I have saved you from those hounds, what say you about my own offer?"

I looked at him and laughed, "Professor, you know that is not going to happen. But everyone thinks it is happening. Your secret is safe with me. If you do not tell them, I will not tell them, and they will not know." We both laughed.

I discovered that many persons were of the impression that I was dating a good number of my lecturers. With the number of names I was rumoured to have been linked to, I fear I would have had no time left on my hands to even grab a meal. I never wasted my time refuting claims or defending myself not even when a few people were bold enough to either directly or indirectly seek verification from me. For me, the choice was simple then, as it is simple now over fifteen years later. It is only the guilty that are afraid. I was not guilty of any of those things people speculated. I owed no one any explanations. I owed myself the truth.

"Loretta, be true to yourself in everything you do. Never give anyone the right to re- write your life script for you. Never let the fear of what others will think about you push you into becoming someone who apologises for everything and who is never able to truly be themselves. Make your choices my daughter after weighing what matters most; which is how your choice will affect the value you place on you. It is the value you place on you, that will determine the value you place on others. It is your true self only that can hold you accountable for the wrongs you do and cause you to change - for change comes from within and is not forced from without. Besides, the more we feed what people think about us with rebuttals, the longer the matter tarries in the public domain."

Those were my father's words to me. They make a lot of sense. That is the reason I never bother to comment on anything I am accused of by society and the same reason I do not indulge in the accusation of others.

Medical school was really interesting. I became the Vice-President of the Medical Students Association after a keenly contested election. At the start of the proceeding, my campaign manager I had at the time, CM, who is still one of my greatest friends till date, advised me to go for Presidency of the association. I told him I was not sure the environment was ready for a female president yet. In hindsight, I was wrong and he was right. CM is one of the few persons who understood my personality. I do not have the personality of a vice. I also cannot sit and watch fraud being committed in my name. I ended up resigning as Vice-President of the association because the President at the time displayed some less than acceptable traits. Time they say heals all wounds and makes sores better. Hopefully, he has turned a better leaf with the passage of time, after all, are we not all work in progress?

I am my father's daughter. I am unapologetic about it.

THE FRIENDS THAT MADE A DIFFERENCE
AND THE HATERS THAT PROPEL

When I was growing up, my father would sit and chat with some of my friends when they came to visit. He was often assessing them and would later tell me his impression of each person in a most objective manner. (The only time he was not objective was to tell me how my legs were the best when my friends and I were all leaving the house and how he was telling my mother that I needed to wear things that set my legs off). My dad was a man who understood the power of reinforcing the good in his children and how to make us feel that we were and still are the real deal.

If my dad did not see some of my friends over a period, he would ask about them and remind me to check on and care for those I call friends. One of his favourite quotes from Shakespeare's Julius Caesar is 'A friend should bear his friend's infirmities.'

I have made many friends on my life journey. They are all very special - each in their own way. Some have spanned decades, others less. Some are still in contact, others have migrated off my radar either by intent or unintentionally as life evolved. Some go to reappear; others go never to be seen again. Some are new and others are yet to appear on my scene. I was raised to understand the meaning of loyalty to one's friends and the fact that everyone will have a flaw, 'perceived' or 'real'.

My friends span all age groups, religion, tribe and race. They traverse societal strata and infiltrate different professions. True about ninety per cent of my friends are males with a smaller ten per cent being females. That just happened. I did not set out for it to be that way. However, it is not difficult to see why it is so skewed if you have read this book, and you got to this page.

There were those friends who rescued me from hunger when I was in University. There were those who made it a point of duty to go beyond me to my family and siblings at home, they provided foodstuffs and gave cash.

I have friends who inspired and still inspire me. There were those who blew hot and cold. Not quite knowing where to belong. The 'frenemies'.

There were the outright haters and I am not naïve to wish there were none. In fact, I know there will always be this group who I am eternally indebted to, because in their own unique way, they propel me unto greater heights.

I will resist the temptation to mention the names or initials of any of my friends or even describe them because that will be causing a third world war storm in my little teacup!

I just want you all to know that you are all dear to me, irrespective of when or how you came into my space. You are treasured and valued and for managing to live with my weirdness and tolerate my excesses, I duff my hat to all of you. You all are the wind beneath my wings.

I am my father's daughter. I am unapologetic about it.

I DO NOT WANT TO MARRY

I had my fair share of kissing frogs and enlightening relationships. After a while, I resolved there was no need to be unequally yoked to some bloke who could not comprehend the 'me' in me.

I could not be bothered by males who felt threatened by any female folk who could employ the grey matter between her ears better than the vacuum between her legs. So I resolved there was no need to marry.

I never told my mother that I was not interested in getting married for many years. The reason was because I knew it would break her heart. At the time, I was strongly determined marriage was not for me as 'I could not suffer fools' and many of the male folk I encountered then, did not tick my box. Then, one day, I summoned courage and told her.

"My enemies are at work!" She screamed. As you would have observed by now, anything my mother could not logically explain was attributed to her enemies. She continued her rant about them, saying, "But they will not succeed. You see how your father has over the years brainwashed your mind? Now Richard is no more and he expects me to fix all of this? Where is my phone, I need to call my Pastor."

Fast forward a few years down the line after that incident and I came home with a boy who had dreadlocks and did not think I was born to be his cook. The dreadlocks did not appeal to my mum and she has never told me this; but I saw and still remember the look in her eyes that implied anything was better than my initial decision not to marry. She quickly accepted the young man.

What I never told her till today though, is that I was the hair twister. I locked my friend's hair – my friend who would eventually become my husband. I do not think Mummy needs to know I am the dreadlock maker because; the ancestors need to earn their well-deserved rest. Do you think I should tell her?

I am my father's daughter. I am unapologetic about it.

SEEKING GREENER PASTURES

While in Nigeria, Douglas, my friend with the locked hair who has been my husband now for the last fifteen years, decided while we were yet friends that he would be a neurosurgeon. I thought that was really cool since I had also considered the specialty until I had a brief stint with neuro-anatomy in medical school and then decided I had to move in a direction opposite the brain.

"Where do you want to do this neurosurgery?" I asked him?

"I know there is no neurosurgery accredited training in Benin now, and I will not go to Ibadan because I am not cut out to gene-flex or lie down at the feet of everyone, so instead of suffering tribal challenge in Ibadan, I rather go to the United Kingdom and struggle with racial challenge."

"Spoken like a true Okor," I said to him, laughing.

"Why not the United States?" I asked?

"Too far," he replied. "Too far. I need to come back to Nigeria. We need to come back. We need to come back and fix things around here in the healthcare sector. Nigerians should not die needlessly."

"Why do I have the feeling that you will only just prolong the time I will spend becoming an Obstetrician and Gynaecologist with this your Neurosurgery?" I asked him?

"You do know that if I were to do my Obstetrics and Gynaecology here in Benin, I will finish in record time?"

His project became my project and true to our vision, we were able to actualise our dreams of coming to the United Kingdom, worked as a team through thick and thin and coming out at the other end in one piece. Each time I reflect on our sojourns in the United Kingdom, I conclude that God's divine intervention played a major role. We were tossed and turned on our life journey by many issues that came one after the other. Many of these events I will save for my next book. A book that will x-ray a whole new chapter of my life when compared to this narrative.

In the years we have been together, there have been the ups and downs, the highs and lows. However, I know daddy will be pleased; I did not marry a man who is threatened by his little girl. Pa. Richard will be happy that Douglas does not consider me competition or an object. I have been lucky to find one of the few men worth his salt, who treasures and values me. Like daddy predicted, this has brought out the very loyal and loving best in me.

I am my father's daughter. I am unapologetic about it.

EPILOGUE

Pa. Richard used to tell me "Each one of us is born for a purpose." We are born into our families and our countries for a reason. It is no co-incidence that we are who we are and born when and where we were born.

It took me a while to understand what he meant then, but now I truly do. The requirement for my life assignment of bettering the lot of my fellow human was that I be groomed the way my dad raised me. I believe all of this was in preparation for the larger assignment I have to do in the future.

It is one thing to mentor and train an individual; it is another thing for the mentee to soak up what is being sowed. I guess my father found a good student of life in me and I on the other hand, was eager to learn at the feet of this master whom nature had bestowed on me.

I do strongly believe that every parent, potential parent, guardian, child or ward that reads this book, will connect with the words of wisdom therein. In our society especially, where the girl child is 'almost often viewed as a second class citizen', my dad ensured that I was insulated from that mentality. He ensured I was raised to understand and appreciate my self-worth. I do not need a father, a brother or a husband, in whose shadow I should abide. If I had these individuals in my life, it was fine. It was no offence. However, I needed first, to be me and to get things on my own merit.

In an in-depth analysis, the significance of what my father did with me, can be likened to be the solution to the bane of some of our societal existence today as nations across the world. It is without doubt, that some nations suffer more than others and that a few have managed to evolve beyond the basal docility of followership, which is a retrogressive factor for growth in any society.

He awoke my consciousness to question his authority. He submerged my docility and very subtly, ignited a vibrancy that he also enabled me to modulate appropriately. To question or interrogate ideas, ideals, processes or systems does not equate disobedience. Rather, it is an indicator or outcome measure of the engagement of individuals with their socio-cultural and economic environment – a reflection of the vibrancy of followership.

A critical examination of this concept, using my story so far as a case study is what I urge every reader to reflect on. This will enable an assessment at the primary unit of society.....which is

the home or family and compare it with what happens in the macro society. What we find is that the negative effects are similar.

When in a home, a family member does as he or she pleases, without any repercussions or questioning by the followers, which in this case are the other members of the same family, then there will be problem. If a man marries a wife who he can oppress at will, because of a power gradient which could be educational, economic or sociocultural, or in some cases, all of the above, then the woman cannot negotiate. She will not be able to interrogate his actions. He will do as he pleases because the followership in that home is not vibrant.

Spare me the 'woman should be submissive' bit of the biblical age-old quote. A woman can be submissive and yet vibrant. A submissive person can interrogate the actions of another to get them to reflect on their actions and not necessarily to upstage or rebel against them.

Now, juxtapose this with the scenario of a man who is married to a wife he cannot oppress because she has a negotiating chip. Her negotiating chip is her education, her economic and financial standing in society and her mindset – how much value she places on herself. Such a man understands that his processes will be interrogated and that his primary constituent is not docile so he will employ some measure of diplomacy and negotiation more than the earlier example on the flip side of this coin.

On a grander scale, let us take these principles now, out of the family unit and apply it to the macro society. Specifically, let us use it as a tool to evaluate the Nigerian situation since Nigeria is the setting for this aspect of my life story. When a people fail to ask questions of their 'rulers' (mind you, not leaders), then 'rulership' runs unhinged and grinds with reckless abandon. It becomes unaccountable and proceeds to acquire an all-supreme toga.

True leadership evolves when leaders have value for human life and are held accountable for their actions by the followers. When the citizenry becomes vibrant and ask those difficult questions that makes those at the helm of affairs sit up, then leadership is kept on its toes. When interrogation of authority is consistent then leadership becomes people conscious. When our society stops its worship of materialism and understands the value of honest and consistent people who make sacrifices to serve their people, then mortgaging the conscience of the very society that belongs to us all cannot be done by a few.

A wise man once said that people are deserving of the leaders they get. In a situation where the status quo has become 'move on as if nothing happens and no one would interrogate the action of rulers' which is what Nigeria has become, what do we expect will happen to such a country?

I want to believe that there are many other parents like Pa. Richard, who caught the vision that we need a paradigm shift. Starting from our homes. We need to raise our children to start asking us questions about what we do, why we do them and if it could have been done any better. They need to learn how to hold us accountable from an early age. Which in effect is what my dad did with me, from day one.

These children too, will then imbibe the value of being held accountable as well. That way, they understand how to objectively question authority and it becomes a life style, which will cascade into improved societal vibrancy that will overrun the present docility of Nigerian followers.

Only then, when our citizenry/followership awakens properly, can we positively evolve past our current state as a people. That is when we will understand the true meaning of leadership, which is 'service to the people'. That is when we will stop thinking that when a Governor tars one road or hugs one citizen or pays salaries when due, it is a favour or a miracle.

Only when Nigerian followership awakens and judders our leadership will true leaders emerge from among us. Our

development is a top bottom and bottom top approach and not a luminal flow in one direction. As I have often said, and I will say here again, only Nigerians can change Nigeria for Nigerians and no one else will fix our nation for us. This is the very reason we need more Pa. Richards (the legacy of Pa. Richard needs to be shared and cultivated), to breed the critical mass of vibrant Nigerians that will spearhead this change.

I am my father's daughter. I remain unapologetic about it.

About The Author

Loretta Oduware Ogboro-Okor, is a United Kingdom trained Obstetrician and Gynaecologist. She has been able to blend her work in the science field of medical practise and research, with being an author, a passionate motivational speaker, women and youth health advocate and educationist as well as a social entrepreneur and an ardent blogger. She set up the Loretta Reveals "borderless motivational space" http://lorettareveals.org in 2015. She also co-founded the Ashanti Graham Health & Education Initiative Foundation (AGHEIF) in 2010 - a charity with the vision "21st Century Health Care for Africa." The charity has made significant progress in enabling capacity development in Nigeria through healthcare training for medical professionals and providing important equipment and hardware for medical institutions.

Loretta earned her MBBS degree from the prestigious University of Benin in Nigeria. She bagged further postgraduate degrees: an MSc in Public Health Research and another in Clinical Education from the Universities of Edinburgh and Sheffield Hallam both in the United Kingdom. She is a member of the Royal College of Obstetricians and Gynaecologist in the United Kingdom and has worked in the National Health Service now, for over 10 years.

Apart from being a woman in the field of science and healthcare provision, her life journey reflects roles in leadership, people motivation, academics, research and advocacy. Loretta is passionate about "Cultural Integration" in African communities as a means to tackling women's Reproductive and Mental Health issues as well as Trafficking. She is dedicated to motivating people; principally those who are migrants from ethnic minority backgrounds to achieving a life of purpose and significance because she understands that having limited use of the common language (in this case English) as well as peculiar cultural sensibilities can be a huge challenge to societal integration for migrant populations-especially women.

This multi-talented family building woman of ancient Benin heritage has been awarded accolades for her voluntary works and community commitments across continents in both United Kingdom and Nigeria.

She is the current President of the University of Benin Alumni Association, United Kingdom Branch.

Contact her via: info@lorettareveals.org or
lorettareveals@gmail.com

Printed in Great Britain
by Amazon